# PRESIDENT WASHINGTON'S DIARIES

1791 TO 1799

TRANSCRIBED AND COMPILED BY

JOS. A. HOSKINS

# Contents

## PUBLISHER'S NOTES

At this far remove of the 21st century, it is difficult to grasp just what it was about Washington that made him the first man of his new nation. You may read many biographies of Washington and still come away wondering.

The Washington of these journals is not the great man but the man attending to various duties as the hero of his country and ex-president. What comes through is a man with specific concerns on his mind.

Ever anxious about finances, you'll read in his diary entries his appraisal of country that he travels through, always with an eye to what it could be worth in land and materials. As a farmer, he notes weather conditions and concerns about the effect of frosts or heat on crops.

Everywhere he went, Washington was the star of his day. Everyone wanted to see him and celebrate him. It's extraordinary how well he seems to have tolerated this, knowing what it meant to the people and to the country. You get a sense in these diaries that he both loved the attention and wearied of it.

It is also remarkable to note the revolving door of visitors to Mount Vernon in the final years. It seems that daily there was someone leaving, someone arriving, and someone staying for dinner or overnight.

Self-conscious about his lack of formal education, Washington was a notoriously bad and inconsistent speller, as you'll see for yourself. He also made use of rather obscure abbreviations that require some decipherment. For example, you'll note the use of "C'ty" for the word city. Sometimes he spelled "which" as "wch" and sometimes as "wh'ch." Of course, these diaries were written for personal use, not for publication. One wonders, however, if he ever had trouble deciphering them himself.

More than half a century after Washington's death, Lincoln and his contemporaries still viewed the first president as a towering figure among all of human history. Today it is hard to separate him

1

from his marble busts. Hopefully you'll find these diaries as one method of accessing Washington the man.

## LINCOLN'S TRIBUTE TO WASHINGTON

Washington is the mightiest name on earth. Long since mightiest in the cause of civil liberty; still mightiest in the moral reformation. On that name a eulogy is expected. It cannot be. To add brightness to the sun or glory to the name of Washington is alike impossible. Let none attempt it. In solemn awe pronounce the name, and in its naked, deathless splendor leave it shining on.

# FOREWORD

The editing and publishing of President Washington's diaries is here undertaken with the view of presenting all that are extant from the year 1791 to 1799. They are fragmentary but very interesting.

The search for the unpublished parts of the diary was instituted for the purpose of proving the fact of President Washington's visit to Guilford County, North Carolina, and its famous battlefield, on his Southern Tour. It was traditional knowledge in the family of the writer, and, while the facts concerning the visit had faded from the minds of all others, it remained firmly fixed with him. It was while pondering over Lossing's Imprint of the Southern Tour that he became convinced that there must be more of the Journal, and that, if found, it would settle the mooted question.

Lossing stopped June 1st, 1791, (Salem, N. C.) My transcription begins where he left off, and takes the President to Guilford Courthouse, on June 2nd, and on through North Carolina and Virginia to Mount Vernon, where he arrived June 12th, and Philadelphia July 6th. At this time Washington was President of the United States.

The trip to Georgetown, to the Federal City and on to Philadelphia began June 27th, 1791. He travelled by way of the upper road through Williamsburgh, Fredericktown, Taney town, Lyttlestown, Hanover (commonly called McAllistertown), Yorktown and Lancaster. He describes the towns and the intervening country. While in the Federal City he conferred with Maj. L'Enfant and Mr. Ellicott, and selected the spots on which the buildings for the Executive Departments and the President's house were to be located. He directed Maj. L'Enfant to change the location of a certain street, so as to leave out a spring (commonly known as the Cool Spring) belonging to Maj. Stoddart.

In 1794 we find him accompanying the army from Philadelphia to the Rendezvous at Carlisle, passing through Norristown, The Trap, Potts Grove, Reading, Meyers-town, Lebanon, Humelstpwn, and Harrisburg. This was the Whiskey Rebellion Campaign. At Bedford he delivered a speech to the insurgents. This speech has probably never been published before. He here received Messrs. Riddick and Tindley, representatives of the insurgents, and their speeches are given in his diary. The President and the army marched thence to the Rendezvous at Bedford, passing Shippensburgh, Green Castle, Williamsport (Maryland,) Cumberland, (Maryland,) Frankfort, and on to Bedford.

In November, 1798, he gives an account of his triumphal progress to Philadelphia, by way of the lower road. On this journey he stopped and was entertained at the Federal City, Bladensburg, Spurriers, Baltimore, Websters, Hartford, Susquehanna, Elkton, Christianna, Wilmington and Chester. At this time he was Commander of the army, with Major Gen'l Alexander Hamilton second in command. This was during the period of the French Imbroglio. General Washington was dined and feted in Philadelphia by President Adams and others. He names his entertainers.

The diary that Washington kept at Mount Vernon is largely interesting because it is an account of the guests who came and went after enjoying his hospitality. The name of each is given, and hundreds are mentioned—the famous people of the day. From another viewpoint this part of the diary is interesting. It shows the painstaking, methodical Washington, in that hardly a day is passed that accurate and careful mention of the weather is not made, the thermometer and barometer readings recorded and the direction of the wind stated. Many of these weather observations have been omitted from this transcript, only enough of them being retained to show Washington's carefulness and diligence in all things. The last entry in the diary (in his own hand) was made December 13th, 1799. He died the following day.

His entire Southern Tour is here presented, beginning at Phila.— March 21, 1791, giving names of scores of towns visited in the states of Pennsylvania, Maryland, Virginia, North Carolina, South Carolina, and Georgia. Many of these are now large towns and cities. This part of the diary is full of local color.

In confirmation of the claims set forth above an editorial from the *Greeensboro Daily News*, under date of February 15th, 1920, and a letter from the Library of Congress are herewith copied and appended.

Editorial *Greensboro Daily News*, Feb. 15th, 1820

"The discovery of the evidence—in the handwriting of the first President—that George Washington visited Guilford County on his southern tour was made by J. A. Hoskins. It is most improbable that the facts were ever published prior to their publication by Mr. Hoskins in the *Daily News* of December 12, 1919. They are certainly unknown to contemporary North Carolina historians, which means that they had not become facts of historical record; it is not therefore too much to say that the circumstances were unknown to history.

It was well enough known that the diary of President Washington lay in the archives of the government at Washington. The contents have been in part edited and published, but for some reason the compiler stopped just short of the circumstances recorded in the diary which are of most personal interest to North Carolina people.

Mr. Hoskins had, to be sure, a starting point. It was traditional knowledge in his family; a part of those spoken records, records transmitted from generation to generation, and which may be implicitly believed, but of which no competent evidence exists. Mr. Hoskins sought long for that evidence, and it finally occurred to him that the diary of the Southern Tour ought to dispose of the matter. He accordingly applied to the Library of Congress, and was furnishing a photostatic copy of the manuscript. There can be no question of its authenticity, and no one questions it; on the contrary, North Carolina historians give Mr. Hoskins credit for the discovery of a rare gem of historical knowledge.

It is this same investigator who has produced the evidence that Dolly Madison was born at New Garden (Guilford College) N. C. and that Andrew Jackson was a resident of the county and a member of the Guilford bar which evidence he had published hitherto in the Daily News, but he has refrained from announcing any of his discoveries until able to clinch them.

It is doubted if the narrative has ever appeared in print until set up by the compositors of this office.

Letter, Oct. 20th, 1920

(From the Library of Congress)

"The assistant chief of the manuscript division reports that everything that we have between June 27, 1791, and December 13th, 1799 has been sent you."

My transcriptions are made from photastat copies of the original notebooks in Washington's own handwriting.

His spelling, abbreviations and punctuation are observed as near as possible.

JOS. A. HOSKINS,

Elmburst Farm, Summerfield, N. C.

November 18th, 1920.

# WASHINGTON'S DIARY

Monday, March 21-1791

Left Philadelphia about 11 o'clock to make a tour through the Southern States. Reached; Chester about 3~ o'c—dined and lodged at Mr. Wythes—In this tour I was accompanied by Maj. Jackson—My equipage and attendance consisted of a chariot and four horses drove in hand—a light baggage waggon and two-four saddle horses besides a led one for myself—and five—to wit—my Valet De Chambre—two footmen, Coachman, and postillion.

March 22.

At half past six o'c we left Chester and breakfasted at Wilmington—crossing Christiana Creek proceeded through New Castle and by the Red Lyon to Buck tavern 13 miles from New Castle and 19 from Wilmington where we dined and lodged.

March 23.

Set off at 6 o'c—breakfasted at Warwick—bated with hay 9 miles farther and dined & lodged at the house of one Worrell's in Chester (town).

March 24.

Left Chestertown about 6 o'c—before nine I arrived at Rock Hall (on Chesapeake Bay) where we breakfasted and immediately after which we began to embark. After 8 o'c P M we made the mouth of Severn River (leading up to Annapolis) but the ignorance of the people on board with respect to the navigation of it ran us aground first on Greenbury point from whence with much exertion and difficulty we got off—and then having no knowledge of the Channel and the night being immensely dark with heavy and variable squalls of wind—constant lightning & tremendous thunder—we soon got aground again on what is called Horne's Point—where finding all efforts in vain and not knowing where we were we remained not knowing what might happen till morning.

March 25.

Having Lain all night in my great coat & Boots in a birth not long enough for me by the head and much cramped, we found ourselves in the morning within about one mile of Annapolis & still fast aground. Whilst we were preparing our Small Boat in order to land in it, a sailing Boat came off to our assistance in wch with the baggage I had on board, I landed—was informed upon my arrival (when 15 guns were fired) that all my other horses arrived safe that embarked at the same time I did, about 8 o'c last night—was waited upon by the Governor (John Eager Howard) as soon as I arrived at Man's Tavern and was engaged by him to dine with the citizens of Annapolis this day at Mann's Tavern, and at his house tomorrow. The first I accordingly did.

March 26

Dined at the governors and went to the assembly in the evening where I stayed till half past 10 o'c.

March 27.

About 9 o'c this morning I left Annapolis under a discharge of Artillery and being accompanied by the Governor, a Mr. Kilty of the Council and Mr. Charles Stuart proceeded on, my Journey for Georgetown. Bated at Queen Ann 13 miles, distant and dined and lodged at Bladensburgh.

March 28.

Left Bladensburgh at half after six and breakfasted at Georgetown about 8—where having appointed the Commissioners under the Residence Law to meet me I found Mr. (Thomas) Johnson one of them (and who is chief Justice of the State) in waiting—and soon after came in David Stuart and Dan'l Carroll, Esq's, the other two— (a few miles out of town I was met by the principal citizens of the place and escorted by them—and dined at Suter's Tavern where I also lodged at a public dinner given by the Mayor and Corporation— previous to which I examined the surveys of Mr. (Andrew) Ellicott who had been sent on to lay out the District of ten miles square for the federal seat; and also the works of Maj. L'Enfant* who had been engaged to examine and make a draught of the grds in the vicinity of Georgetown and Carrollsburgh on the Eastern branch.

*Pierre "Peter" Charles L'Enfant (1754–1825) was a French-born American architect and civil engineer best known for designing the layout of the streets of Washington, D.C.—Ed. 2016*

March 29.

Finding the interests of the Land owners about Georgetown and those about Carrollsburgh much at variance and that their fears and jealousies of each were counteracting the public purposes and might prove injurious to its best interest whilst if properly managed they might be made to subserve it—I requested them to meet me at six o'c this afternoon at my lodgings which they accordingly did—dined at Forrest's today with the Commissioners & others.

March 30

The parties to whom I addressed myself yesterday evening having taken the matter into consideration saw the propriety of my observations and that whilst they were contending for the shadow they might loose the substance; and therefore mutually agreed and entered into articles to surrender for public purposes one half of the land they severally possiessed within bounds which were designated as necessary for the City to stand.—This business being thus happily finished and some directions given to the Commissioners, the surveyor and engineer with respect to mode of laying out the district—surveying the grounds for the city and forming them into lots. I left Georgetown-dined in Alexandria and reached Mt. Vernon in the evening.

Thursday, March 31st.

From this time until 7th of April I remained at Mt. V[ernon]. visiting my Plantations every day.

Thursday, 7—April

Recommenced my journey with Horses apparently much refreshed and in good spirits.

In attempting to cross the ferry at Colchester with the four horses hitched to the Chariot by the neglect of the person who stood before them, one of the leaders got overboard when the boat was in swimming water and 50 yards from the shore—with much difficulty he escaped drowning before he could be disengaged—His struggling frightened the others' in such a manner that one after another and in quick succession they all got overboard harnessed and fastened as they were and with the utmost difficulty they were saved & the Carriage escaped being dragged after them, as the whole of it happened in swimming water & at a distance from the shore—Providencially, indeed miracously, by the exertions of the people who put off in Boats & jumped into the River as soon as the Batteau was forced into wading water—no damage was sustained by the horses, Carriage or Harness.

Proceeded to Dumfries where I dined, after which I visited & drank Tea with my Niece Mrs. Thos. Lee.

Friday, 8th.

Set out about 6 o'clock—breakfasted at Stafford Court House—and dined and lodged at my Sister Lewi's in Fredericksburg. *

*His sister Elizabeth married Colonel Fielding Lewis. His son, Lawrence Lewis, was Washington's favorite nephew. He married Nellie Custis, Mrs. Washington's granddaughter, and resided with her at Mount Vernon at the time of Washington's death.

Saturday, 9th.

Dined at an entertainment given by the Citizens of the town. Received and answered an address from the Corporation.

Was informed by Mr. Jno. Lewis, who had, not long since been in Richmond, that Mr. Patrick Henry avowed his interest in the Yazoo Company;* and made him a tender of admission in to it, which he declined—but asking if the Company did not expect the Settlement of the lands would be disagreeable to the Indians was answered by Mr. Henry that the Co intended to apply to Congress for protection—which if not granted they would have recourse to their own means to protect the settlement. That General Scott had a certain quantity of Land (I think 40,000 acres in the Company's grant & was to have the command of the force which was to make the establishment—and more over—that General Muhlenburg had offered £1000 for a certain part of the grant—the quantity I do not recollect if it was mentioned to me.

*The first legislature of Georgia, after the adoption of the Federal Constitution undertook to sell out, to three private companies, the pre-emption right to vast tracts of land west of the Chattahoochee River, unmindful of any rightful claim of the Indians. They were called the Yazoo Land Companies. They sold to the South Carolina Yazoo Company 5,000,000 acres for $66,964; to the Virginia Yazoo Company 7,000,000 acres for $93,742; and to the Tennessee Yazoo Company, 3,500,000 acres for $46,875. These companies not complying with the requirements of the sale, a succeeding legislature declared the bargain a nullity. Some of the purchasers contested the claims, and litigations arose, which became still more complicated when the same lands were sold to other companies.*

Sunday, 10th.

Left Fredericsburg about 6 o'clock—myself, Majr. Jackson and one servant breakfasted at General Spotswood*—the rest of my Servants continued on to Todd's Ordinary where they also breakfasted. Dined at the Bowling Green—and lodged at Kenner's Tavern 14 miles farther—in all 35 m.

*Alexander Spotswood, an officer in the continental army. He and Washington were intimate friends, and frequently corresponded on agricultural subjects.*

Monday, 11th.

Took an early breakfast at Kenner's—bated at one Rawling's half way between that & Richmd and; dined at the latter about 3 o'clock.—On my arrival was saluted by the Cannon of the place—waited on by the Governor* and other Gentlemen—and saw the City illuminated at night.

*Henry Lee (1756-1818) was the 9th Governor of Virginia and the son of Washington's first love—Lucy Grymes, the "Lowland Beauty" of whom he was enamored when only sixteen years of age. Lee was the celebrated leader of the "Legion" in the Southern campaigns, known as "Light Horse Henry Lee," and was the father of Confederate General Robert E. Lee.—Ed. 2016*

Tuesday 12th.

In company with the Governor—The Directors of the James River Navigation Company*—the Manager & many other Gentlemen—I viewed the Canal, Sluces Locks, & other works between the City of Richmond & Westham.—These together have brought the navigation to within a mile and half, or mile and 3/4 of the proposed Bason from which the Boats by means of Locks are to communicate with the tide water navigation below.—The Canal is of sufficient depth everywhere—but in places not brought to its proper width; it seems to be perfectly secure against Ice, Freshes & drift wood—The locks at the head of these works are simple—altogether of hewn stone, except the gates & cills—and very easy & convenient to work—there are two of them, each calculated to raise and lower 6 feet—they cost according to the Manager's, Mr. Harris acct about £3000 but I could see nothing in them to require such a sum to erect them.—The Sluces in the River between the locks and the mouth of the Canal are well graduated and easy of assent—To complete the Canal from the point to which it is now opened, and the Locks at the foot of them, Mr. Harris thinks will require 3 years.

*Washington was president of this company. It had been formed several years before, for the purpose of promoting the internal commerce of the State.

Received an address from the Mayor, Aldermen & Common Council of the City of Richmond at three o'clock, & dined with the Governor at 4 o'clock.

In the course of my inquiries—chiefly from Colo. Carrington*—I cannot discover that any discontents prevail among the people at large, at the proceedings of Congress.—The conduct of the Assembly respecting the assumption† he thinks is condemned by them as intemperate & unwise—and he seems to have no doubt but that the Excise law—as it was called—may be executed without difficulty—nay more, that it will become popular in a little time—His duty as Marshal having carried him through all parts of the State lately, and of course given him the best means of ascertaining the temper & disposition of its Inhabitants—he thinks them favorable towards the General Government—& that they only require to have matters explained to them in order to obain their full assent to the measure adopted by it.

*Colonel Edward Carrington, who was a meritorious officer in the campaigns in the South during the Revolution. He was now active as a United States marshal for a large district in Virginia.*

†*A part of Treasury Secretary Alexander Hamilton's financial scheme for the United States was the assumption of the respective States debts by the general Government. This gave rise to violent opposition, and was the chief cause of Jefferson's bitter hostility to Hamilton. Out of the party feelings engendered by the assumption scheme grew the Republican party, and during the latter years of Washington's administration gave him much trouble because of the unkind spirit of opposition to the measures of his government.*

Wednesday, 13th

Fixed with Colo. Carrington (the supervisor of the district) the surveys of Inspection for the District of this State & named the characters for them—an acct of which was transmitted to the Secretary of the Treasury.

Dined at & public entertainment given by the Corporation of Richmond.

The buildings in this place have increased a good deal since I was here last, but they are not of the best kind—the number of Souls in the City are—.

Thursday, 14th.

Left Richmond after an early breakfast—& passing through Manchester received a Salute from cannon & an Escort of Horse under the command of Captn David Meade Randolph as far as Osbornes* when I was met by the Petersburg Horse & escorted to that place & partook of a Public dinner given by the Mayor & Corporation and went to an Assembly in the evening for the occasion at which there were between 60 & 70 ladies.

*A point between Richmond and Petersburgh, where troops under Benedict Arnold, and the republicans, had a severe skirmish in April, 1781. A prisoner captured by Arnold at that time was asked by him, "If the Americans should catch me, what would they do with me?" The Soldier promptly replied, "They would bury with military honors the leg which was wounded at Quebec and Saratoga, and hang the remainder of you upon a gibbet."*

Petersburgh which is said to contain near 3000 Souls is well situated for trade at present, but when the James River navigation is completed and the cut from Elizabeth River to Pasquotank effected it must decline & that very considerably.—At present it receives at the Inspections nearly a third of the Tobacco exported from the whole State besides a considerable quantity of Wheat and flour— much of the former being Manufactured at the Mills near the Town—Chief of the buildings, in this town are under the hill & unpleasantly situated, but the heights around it are agreeable.

The road from Richmond to this place passes through a poor country principally covered with Pine except the interval lands on the River which we left on our left.

Friday, 15th.

Having suffered very much by the dust yesterday—and finding that parties of horse, & a number of other Gentlemen were intending to attend me part of the way today, I caused their enquiries respecting the time of my setting out, to be answered that, I should endeavor to do it before eight o'clock; but I did it a little after five, by which means I avoided the inconvenience above mentioned.

I came twelve miles to breakfast, at one Jesse Lee's, a tavern newly set upon a small scale, and 15 miles farther to dinner; and where I lodged, at the House of one Oliver, which is a good one for horses, and where there are tolerable clean beds.—For want of proper stages I could go no farther.—The Road along which I travelled today is through a level piney Country, until I came to Nottoway,* on which there seems to be some good land, the rest is very poor & seems scarce of Water.

Finding that the two horses wch drew my baggage wagon were rather too light for the draught; and, (one of them especially) losing his flesh fast, I engaged two horses to be at this place this evening to carry it to the next stage 20 miles off in the morning, and sent them on led to be there ready for me.

Saturday, 16th.

Got into my Carriage a little after 5 o'clock, and travelled thro' a cloud of dust until I came within two or three miles of Hix's ford when it began to Rain.—Breakfasted at one Andrews' a small but decent House about a mile after passing the ford (or rather the bridge) over Meherrin River.—Although raining moderately, but with appearances of breaking up, I continued my journey—induced to it by the crowds which were coming in to a general Muster at the Court House of Greenville, who would I presumed soon have made the HO. I was in too noizy to be agreeable.—I had not however rode two miles before it began to be stormy, & to rain violently which, with some intervals, it contin'd to do the whole afternoon.—The uncomfortableness of it, for Men & Horses, would have induced me to put up; but the only inn short of Hallifax having no stables in wch the horses could be comfortable, & no Rooms or beds which appeared tolerable, & everything else having a dirty appearance, I was compelled to keep on to Hallifax; 27 miles from Andrews—48 from Olivers—and 75 from Petersburgh—

At this place (i e. Halifax) I arrived about six o'clock, after crossing the Roanoke; on the South bank of which it stands.

This river is crossed in flat Boats which take in a Carriage & four horses at once.—At this time, being low, the water was not rapid but at times it must be much so, as it frequently overflows its banks which appear to be at least 25 ft perpendicular height.

The lands upon the River appear rich, & the low grounds of considerable width—but those which lay between the different Rivers—namely Appomattox, Nottaway, Meherrin and Roanoke are all alike flat, poor & covered principally with pine timber.

It has already been observed that before the Rain fell, I was travelling in a continued cloud of dust—but after it had rained some time, the Scene was reversed, and my passage was through water; so level are the Roads.

From Petersburg to Halifax (in sight of the Road) are but few good Houses, with small appearance of wealth.—

The lands are cultivated in Tobacco—Corn—Wheat & Oats, but Tobacco and the raising of Porke for market, seems to be the principal dependence of the Inhabitants; especially towards the Roanoke—Cotton & Flax are also raised but not extensively.

Hallifax is the first town I came to after passing the line between the two States, and is about 20 miles from it.—To this place vessels by the aid of Oars and Setting poles are brought for the produce which comes to this place, and others along the River; and may be carried 8 or 10 miles higher to the falls which are neither great nor of much extent;—above these (which are called the great falls) there are others; but none but what may with a little improvement be passed. This town stands upon high ground; and it is the reason given for not placing it at the head of the navigation there being none but low ground between- it and the falls—It seems to be in a decline & does not it is said contain a thousand Souls.

Sunday, 17th.

Col. Ashe, 105 the Represntative of the district in which this town stands, and several other Gentlemen called upon, and invited me to partake of a dinner which the inhabitants were desirous of seeing me at & excepting it dined with them accordingly.

*John B. Ashe, a soldier of the Revolution under General Greene, a member of the Continental Congress in 1787, a representative in the Federal Congress from 1790 to 1793, and afterwards elected governor of the State. He died before entering upon the duties of the office.*

Monday 18th.

Set out by six o'clock—dined at a small house kept by one Slaughter, 22 miles from Hallifax and lodged at Tarborough 14 miles further.

This place is less than Hallifax, but more lively and thriving; it is situated on Tar River which goes into Pamlico Sound and is crossed at the Town by means of a bridge a great height from the water, and not withstanding the freshes rise sometimes nearly to the arch.— Com, Porke, and some Tar are the exports from it. We were recd, at this place by as good a salute as could be given by one piece of artillery.

17

Tuesday, 19th.

At 6 o'clock I left Tarborough accompanied by some of the most respectable people of the place for a few miles—dined at a trifling place called Greenville 25 miles distant—lodged at one Allan's 14 miles further a very indifferent house without stabling which for the first time since I commenced my Journey were obliged to stand without a cover.

Greenville is on Tar River and the exports the same as from Tarborough with a greater proportion of Tar—for the lower down the greater number of Tar makers are there—This article is contrary to all ideas one would entertain on the subject, rolled as Tobacco by an axis which goes through both heads—one horse draws two barrels in this manner.

Wednesday, 20th.

Left Allan's before breakfast, & under a misapprehension went to a Col. Allen's, supposing it to be public house; where we were very kindly & well entertained without knowing it was at his expense, until it was too late to rectify the mistake.—After breakfasting and feeding our horses here, we proceeded on & crossing the River Nuse 11 miles further, arrived in Newbern to dinner.

At this ferry which is 10 miles from Newbern, we were met by a, small party of Horse; the district Judge (Mr. Sitgreave) and many of the principal Inhabitants of

*John Sitgreave was a resident of Newbern, and had been an officer in the war for Independence. He was a member of the Continental Congress in 1784, of his State Legislature in 1787 and was made United States District Judge.*

Newbern, who conducted us into town to exceeding good lodgings—It ought to have been mentioned that another small party of horse under one Simpson met us at Greenville, and in spite of every endeavor which could comport with decent civility, to excuse myself from it, they would attend me to Newbern.—Col Allen did the same.

This town is situated at the confluence of the Rivers Nuse & Trent, and though low is pleasant. Vessels drawing more than 9 feet water cannot get up loaded.—It stands on a good deal of ground but the buildings are sparce and altogether of Wood—some of which are large & look well—The number of Souls are about 2000.—Its exports consist of Corn, Tobacco, Pork.—but principally of Naval Stores & lumber.

Thursday, 21st.

Dined with the Citizens at a public dinner given by them; and went to a dancing assembly in the evening—both of which was at what they call the Pallace—formerly the Government House & a good brick building but now hastening to Ruins.—The Company at both was numerouse at the latter there were abt. 70 ladies.

This town by Water is about 70 miles from the Sea—but in a direct line to the entrance to the River not over 35—and to the nearest Seaboard not more than 20, or 25,—Upon the River Nuse, & 80 miles above Newbern, the Convention of the State that adopted the federal Constitution made choice of a spot, or rather district within which to fix their Seat of Government; but it being lower than the back Members (of the Assembly) who hitherto have been most numerous inclined to have it they have found means to obstruct the measure—but since the Cession of their Western territory it is supposed that the matter will be revived to good effect.

Friday, 22d.

Under an Escort of horse, and many of the principal Gentlemen of Newbern I recommenced my journey—dined at a place called Trenton which is the head of the boat navigation of the River Trent, wch is crossed at this place on a bridge—and lodged at one Shrine's 10 m farther—both indifferent Houses. Sat. 23. Breakfasted at one Everett's 12 m—bated at a Mr. Foy's 12 m farther & lodged at one Sage's 20 m beyd it—all indifferent houses.

Sunday, 24th.

Breakfasted at indifferent House about 13 miles from Sage's—and three miles further met a party of Light Horse from Wilmington;

and after these a Commee. & other Gentlemen of the Town; who came out to escort me in to it and at which I arrived under a federal salute at very good lodgings prepared for me, about two o'clock—at these I dined with the Commee whose company I asked.

The whole Road from Newbern to Wilmington (except in a few places of small extent) passes through the most barren country I ever beheld; especially in the parts nearest the latter; which is no other than a bed of white sand. In places however, before we came to these, if the ideas of poverty could be separated from the Sand, the appearances of it are agreeable, resembling a lawn well covered with evergreens, and a good verdure below from a broom or course grass which having sprung since the burning of the Woods had a neat and handsome look especially as there were parts entirely open—and others with ponds of water, which contributed not a little to the beauty of the scene.

Wilmington is situated on the Cape Fear River, about 30 miles by water from its mouth, but much less by land—It has some good houses pretty compactly built—The whole undr a hill; which is formed entirely of sand.—The number of Souls in it amount by the enumeration to about 1,000, but it is agreed on all hands that the Census in this State has been very inaccurately & Shamefully taken by the Marshall's deputies; who, instead of going to Peoples houses, & there on the spot, ascertaining the Nos.; have advertised a meeting of them at certain places, by which means those who did not attend (and it seems many purposely avoided doing it, some from an apprehension of its being introductory of a tax, & others from religious scruples) have gone with their families, unnumbered—In other instances, it is said these deputies have taken their information from the Captains of Militia Companies; not only as to the men on their Muster Rolls, but of the Souls, in their respective families; which at best, must in a variety of cases, be mere conjecture whilst all those who are not ow their lists—Widows and their families &c pass unnoticed.

Wilmington, unfortunately for it, has a Mud bank—miles below, over which not more than 10 feet water can be brought at common tides, yet it is said vessels of 250 Tons have come up. The qty of

Shipping, which load here annually, amounts to about 1200 Tons.— The exports consist chiefly of Naval Stores and lumber.—Some Tobacco, Corn, Rice, & flax seed with Porke.—It is at the head of the tide navigation, but inland navigation may be extended 115 miles farther to and above Fayetteville which is from Wilmington 90 miles by land, & 115 by water as above.—Fayetteville is a thriving place containing near— Souls—6000 Hhds [hogsheads] of Tobacco, & 3000 Hhds of Flax Seed have been reed, at it in the course of the year.

Monday, 25th.

Dined with the Citizens of the place at a public dinner given by them—Went to a Ball in the evening at which there were 62 ladies— illuminations, Bonfires, &c.

Tuesday, 26th. Apr.

Having sent my carriage across the day before, I left Wilmington about 6 o'clock, accompanied by most of the Gentlemen of the Town, and breakfasting at Mr. Ben. Smith's lodged at one Russ' 25 miles from Wilmington.—An indifferent House—

Wednesday—April 27th, 1791

Breakfasted at Willm Gause's a little out of the direct Road 14 miles—crossed the boundary line between No & South Carolina abt half after 12 o'clock which is 10 miles from Gause's—dined at a private house (one Cochran's) about 2 miles farther—and lodged at Mr. Vareen's 14 miles more and 2 miles short of the long bay.—To this house we were directed as a Tavern, but the proprietor of it either did not keep one, or would not acknowledge it—we therefore were entertained) (& very kindly) without being able to make compensation.

Thursday, 28th.

Mr. Vareen piloted us across the Swash (which at high water is impassible, & at times, by the shifting of the Sands is dangerous) on the long Beach of the Ocean; and it being at a proper time of the tide we passed along it with ease and celerity to the place of quitting it, which is estimated 16 miles—five miles farther we got dinner & fed our horses at a Mr. Pauley's a private house, no public one being on the Road;—and being met on the Road, & kindly invited by a Doctor Flagg to his house, we lodged there; it being about 10 miles from Pauley's & 33 from Vareen's.

Friday, 29th.

We left Doctr Flagg's about 6 o'clock, and arrived at Captn Wm. Alstons on the Waggamau to Breakfast.

Captn Alston is a Gentleman of large fortune and esteemed one of the neatest Rice planters in the State of So Carolina and a proprietor of the most valuable ground for the culture of this article.—His house which is large new, and elegantly furnished stands on a sand hill, high for the Country, with his Rice fields below; the contrast of which, with the lands back of it, and the Sand & piney barrens through which we had passed is scarcely to be conceived.

At Captn. Alston's we were met by General Moultree, Colo Washington* & Mr. Rutledge (son of the present Chief Justice of So Carolina) who had come out that far to escort me to town.—We dined and lodged at this Gentlemen's and Boats being provided we the next morning.

*Colonel William Washington (1752-1810), the eminent cavalry officer in the southern campaign in the Revolution. He had invited the President several months before he commenced his journey, to accept the hospitalities of his house in Charleston. "I cannot," replied the President, "without involving myself in inconsistency; as I have determined to pursue the same plan in my Southern—as I did in my Eastern visit, which was not to incommode any private family by taking up my quarters with them during my journey. It leaves me unencumbered by engagements, and by a uniform adherence to it, I shall avoid giving umbrage to any, by declining all such invitations."

Saturday, 30th.

Crossed the Waggamau [Waccamaw] to Georgetown by descending the River three miles—at this place we were reed, under a Salute of Cannon, & by a Company of Infantry handsomely uniformed.—I dined with the Citizens in public; and in the afternoon, was introduced to upwards of 50 ladies who had assembled (at a Tea party) on the occasion.

George Town seems to be in the shade of Charleston—It suffered during the War by the British, having had many of its Houses burnt.—It is situated on a pininsula betwn the River Waccamaw & Sampton Creek about 15 miles from the Sea—a bar is to be passed, over which not more than 12 feet of water can be brot except at Spring tides; which (tho' the Inhabitants are willing to entertain different ideas,) must ever be a considerable let to its importance; especially if the cut between the Santee & Cooper Rivers, should ever be accomplished.

The inhabitants of this place (either unwilling or unable) could give no account of the number of Souls in it, but I should not compute them at more than 5 or 600.—Its chief export, Rice.

Sunday, May 1st.

Left Georgetown about 6 o'clock and crossing the Santee Creek at the Town, and the Santee River 12 miles from it, at Lynch's Island, we breakfasted and dined at Mrs. Horry's about 15 miles from Georgetown & lodged at the plantation of Mr. Manigold* about 19 miles farther.

*Manigualt, a family of South Carolina that owned multiple plantations. The father, Peter, was the wealthiest person in British North America in 1770.—Ed. 2016

Monday, 2d.

Breakfasted at the Country seat of Govr. Pinckney* about 18 miles from our lodging place, & then came to the ferry at Haddrel's point, 6 miles further, where I was met by the Recorder of the City, Genl Pinckney & Edward Rutledge, Esq in a 12 oared barge rowed by 12 American Captains of Ships, most elegantly dressed.—There were a great many other Boats with Gentlemen and ladies in them;—and two Boats with Music; all of whom attended me across, and on the passage were met by a number of others.—As we approached the town a salute with artillery commenced, and at the Wharf I was met by the Governor, the Lt. Governor, the Intendt of the City;—the two

Senators of the State, Wardens of the City—Cincinnati, &c. &c and conducted to the Exchange where they passed by in procession—from thence I was conducted in like manner to my lodgings—after which I dined at the Governors (in what he called a private way) with 15 or 18 Gentlemen.

*Charles Pinckney, one of the delegates in the convention that framed the Federal Constitution. He was governor of his State at three different periods; a Senator of the United States, and minister to Spain*

It may as well in this as in any other place, be observed, that the Country from Wilmington through which the Road passes, is, except in very small spots, much the same as what has alredy been described; that is to say, sand & pine barrens—with very few inhabitants—we were indeed informed that at some distance from the Road on both sides the land was of a better quality, & thicker settled, but this could only be on the Rivers & larger waters—for a perfect sameness seems to run through all the rest of the Country—on these—especially the swamps and low lands on the Rivers, the Soil is very rich; and productive when reclaimed; but to do this is both laborious and expensive.—The Rice planters have two modes of watering their fields—the first by the tide—the other by resurvoirs drawn from the adjacent lands.—The former is best because most certain.—A crop without either is precarious—because a drought may not only injure, but destroy it.—Two and an half and 3 barrels to the Acre is esteemed a good Crop and 8 or 10 Barrels, for each grown hand is very profitable; but some have 12 & 14, whilst 5 or 6 is reckoned the average production of a hand—a barrel contains about 600 weight and the present price is about 10|6 & 11| Sterg pr. 100.

The lodgings provided for me in this place were very-good, being the furnished house of a Gentleman at present in the Country; but occupied by a person placed there on purpose to accommodate me, & who was paid in the same manner as any other letter of lodgings would have been paid.

Tuesday, 3rd.

Breakfasted with Mrs. Rutledge (the Lady of the Chief Justice of the State who was on the Circuits) and dined with the Citizens at a public dinr given by them at the Exchange.

Was visited about 2 o'clock by a great number of the most respectable ladies of Charleston—the first honor of the kind I had ever experienced and it was as flattering as it was singular.

Wednesday, 4th.

Dined with the Members of the Cincinnati, and in the evening went to a very elegant dancing Assembly at the Exchange—At which were 256 elegantly dressed & handsome ladies.

In the forenoon, (indeed before breakfast today) I visited and examined the lines of attack & defence of the City and was satisfied that the defence was noble & honorable altho' the measure was undertaken upon wrong principles and impolitic.*

Thursday, 5th.

Visited the works of Fort Johnson James' Island, and Fort Moultree on Sullivans Island;—both of which are in Ruins, and scarcely a trace of the latter left—the former quite fallen in.

Dined with a very large company at the Governor's & in the evening went to a Concert at the Exchange at wch there were at least 400 ladies in the number & appearance of wch exceeded any thing of the kind I had ever seen.

Friday, 6th.

Viewed the town on horseback by riding through most of the principal Streets.

Dined at Majr. Butler's and went to a Ball in the evening at the Governors where there was a select Company of ladies.

Saturday, 7th.

Before break (fast) I visited the Orphan House at which there were one hundred & seven boys & girls—This appears to be a charitable institution and under good management—I also viewed the City from balcony of

25

— Church from whence the whole is seen in in one view and to advantage, the Gardens & green trees which are interspersed adding much to the beauty of the prospect.

Charleston stands on a Pininsula between the Ashley & Cooper Rivers and contains about 1600 dwelling houses and nearly 16,000 Souls of which about 8000 are white—It lies low with unpaved streets (except footways) of sand. There are a number of very good houses of Brick & wood but most of the latter—The Inhabitants are wealthy—Gay—& hospitable; appear happy and satisfied with the Genl. Government. A cut is much talked of between the Ashley & Santee Rivers but it would seem I think, as if the accomplishment of the measure was not very near—It would be a great thing for Charleston if it could be effected.—The principal exports from this place is Rice, Indigo, and Tobacco; of the last from 5 to 8000 Hhds have been exported, 'and of the first from 80 to 120,000 Barrels.

Sunday, 8th.

Went to Crowded Churches in the morning & afternoon to— in the morning &— in the afternoon. Dined with General Moultree.

Monday, 9th.

At six o'clock I recommenced my journey for Savanna; attended by the Corps of the Cincinnati and most of the principal Gentlemen of the City as far as the bridge over Ashley River, where we breakfasted, and proceeded to Colo W. Washington's at Sandy-hill with a select party of particular friends—distant from Charleston 28 miles.

Tuesday, 10th.

Took leave of all my friends and attendants at this place (except General Moultree & Majr. Butler the last of whom intended to accompany me to Savanna, and the other to Purisburgh [Purysburg]. at which I was met by Boats,) & breakfasting at Judge Bee's 12 mlies from Sandy Hill, lodged at Mr. Obrian Smith's 18 or 20 further on.

Wednesday, 11th.

After an early breakfast at Mr. Smith's we road 20 miles to a place called Pokitellico [Pocotaligo] where a dinner was provided by the Parishioners of Prince William for my reception, and an address from them was presented and answered.—After dinner we proceeded 16 miles farther to Judge Hayward's where we lodged, &, as also at Mr. Smith's were kindly and hospitably entertained.—My going to Colo Washington's is to be ascribed to motives of friendship & relationship; but to Mr. Smith's & Judge Haywards to those of necessity; their being no public houses on the Road and my distance to get to these private ones increased at least 10 or 12 miles between Charleston and Savanna.

Thursday, 12th.

By five o'clock we set out from Judge Hayward's, and road to Purisburgh 22 miles to Breakfast.

At that place I was met by Messrs. Jones, Colo Habersham, Mr. Jno. Houston, Genl. Mc.Intosh and Mr. Clay,* A Comee from the City of Savanna to conduct me thither.

*Noble Wimberly Jones, Joseph Habesham, John Houston, Lachlin McIntosh, and Joseph Clay, all eminent patriots during the Revolution.

Boats also were ordered there by them for my accommodation; among which a handsome 8 oared barge rowed by 8 American Capt.ns attended.—In my way down the River I called upon Mrs. Green the Widow of the deceased Genl. Green,* (at a place called Mulberry Grove) & asked her how she did?—At this place (2 miles from Purisburgh) my horses and Carriages were landed, and had 12 miles farther by land to Savana.—The wind & tide being both agst us, it was 6 o'clock before we reached the City where we were received under every demonstration that could be given of joy & respect.—We were Seven hours making the passage which is often performed in 4, tho' the computed distance is 25 miles—Illumns at night.

*The State of Georgia gave General Nathaniel Greene quite a large tract of land in testimony of appreciation for his services in the Southern campaigns of the Revolution. He went to Georgia in 1785, to look after his estate; while walking one day, in June, 1786, without an umbrella, he was *"sun struck," and died on the 19th of that month, at the age of forty-six years. His widow occupied the property until her death. There, under the roof of that hospitable lady, in 1792 or '93, Eli Whitney, the inventor of the cotton-gin, planned and constructed his first machine; and at that home, in 1807, the daughter of General Greene, received the brass cannon, captured at Eutaw Springs, which Congress voted to her father.*

I was conducted by the Mayor and Warden to very good lodging which had been provided for the occasion, and partook of a public dinner given by the Citizens at the

Coffee Room.—At Purisburgh I parted with Genl. Moultree.

Friday, 13th.

Dined with the Members of the Cincinnati at a public dinner given at the same place—and in the evening went to a dancing Assembly at which there was about 100 well dressed & handsome ladies.

Saturday, 14th.

A little after 6 o'clock, in Company with Genl. McIntosh, Genl. Wayne, the Mayor and many others (principal Gentlemen of the City,) I visited the City, and the attack & defence of it in the year 1779, under the combined forces of France and the United States, commanded by the Count de Estang & Genl. [Benjamin] Lincoln.— To form an opinion of the attack at this distance of time, and the change which has taken place in the appearance of the ground by the cutting away of the woods, &c is hardly to be done with justice to the subject; especially as there is remaining scarcely any of the defences.

Dined today with a number of the Citizens (not less than 200) in an elegant Bower erected for the occasion on the Bank of the River below the Town.—In the evening there was a tolerable good display of fireworks.

Sunday, 15th.

After morning Service, and receiving a number of visits from the most respectable ladies of the place (as was the case yesterday) I set out for Augusta, Escorted beyd the limits of the City by most of the

Gentlemen in it, and dining at Mulberry Grove the Seat of Mrs. Green—lodged at one Spencers—distant 15 miles.

Savanna stands upon what may be called high ground for this Country—It is extremely Sandy wch. makes the walking very disagreeable; & the houses uncomfortable in warm & windy weather, as they are filled with dust whenever these happen.—The town on 3 sides is surrounded with cultivated Rice fields which have a rich and luxuriant appearance. On the 4th or backside it is a fine sand.—The harbour is said to be very good, & often filled with square rigged vessels, but there is a bar below over which not more than 12 water can be brot except at sprg tides.—The tide does not flow above 12 or 14 miles above the City though the River is swelled by it more than double that distance.—Rice & Tobacco (the last of wch is greatly increasing) are the principal Exports—Lumber & Indigo are also Exported, but the latter is on the decline, and it is supposed by Hemp & Cotton.—Ship timber, viz: live Oak & Cedar, is (and may be more so) valuable in the exptn.

Monday, 16th.

Breakfasted at Russells—15 miles from Spencer's—dined at Garnets 19 further & lodged at Pierces 8 miles more, in all 42—miles today.

Tuesday, 17th.

Breakfasted at Spinner's 17 miles—dined at Lamberts 13—and lodged at Waynesborough (wch was coming 6 miles out of our way) 14, in all 43 miles—Waynesborough is a small place, but the Seat of the Court of Burkes County—6 or 8 dwelling houses is all it contains;—an attempt is making (without much apparent effect) to establish an Academy at it as is the case also in all the counties.

Wednesday, 18th.

Breakfasted at Fulcher's 15 miles from Waynesborough; and within 14 miles of Augusta met the Govor. (Telfair), Judge Walton,* the Attorney Genl. & most of the principal Gentlemen of the place; by whom I was escorted into the Town, & reed, under a discharge of Artillery—the distance I came today was about 32 miles—Dined with a large Company at the Governors, & drank Tea there with many well dressed Ladies.

*George Walton, one of the signers of the Declaration of Independence. A fine monument stands in Augusta, erected to the memory of Walton and his Georgia colleagues who signed that document.*

The road from Savanna to Augusta is, for the most part through Pine barrens; but more uneven than I had been accustomed to since leavg. Petersburgh in Virginia, especially after riding about 30 miles from the City of that name; here & there indeed, a piece of Oak land is passed on this Road, but of small extent & by no means of the first quality.

Thursday, 19th.

Received & answered an Address from the Citizens of Augusta;—dined with a large Company of them at their Court Ho.—and went to an Assembly in the evening at the Academy; at which there were between 60 & 70 well dressed ladies.

Friday, 20th.

Viewed the Ruins, or rather small Remns of the Works which had been erected by the British during the War and taken by the Americans.—Also the falls, which are about 2 miles above the Town; and the Town itself.

These falls (as they are called) are nothing more than rapids.—They are passable in their present state by boats with skillful hands, but may at a very small expence be improved, by removing a few rocks only, to streighten the passage.—Above them there is a good boat navigation for many miles; by which the produce may be, & in some measure is, transported.—At this place, i e the falls, the good lands begin; & encrease in quality to the westward & No ward—All below them, except the interval lands on the Rivers and Rice Swamps which extend from them, the whole Country is a Pine barren.—The town of Augusta is well laid out with wide & spacious Streets.—It stands on a large area of a perfect plain but is not yet thickly built tho' surprisingly so for the time; for in 1783 there were not more than half a dozen dwelling houses; now there are not less than— containing about— Souls of which about— are blacks.—It bids fair to be a large Town being at the head of the present navigation, & a fine Country back of it for support, which is settling very fast by Tobacco planters.—The culture of which article in encreaseing very fast, and bids fair to be the principal export from the State; from this part of it, it certainly will be so.

Augusta, though it covers more ground than Savanna, does not contain as many Inhabitants the latter having by the late census between 14 & 1500 hundred whites and about 800 black.

Dined at a private dinner with Govr. Telfair to day; and gave him dispatches for the Spanish Govr of East Florida, respecting the Countenance given by that Govemt to the fugitive Slaves of the Union—wch dispatches were to be forwarded to Mr. Seagrove, Collector of St. Mary's, who was requested to be the bearer of them, and instructed to make arrangements for the prevention of these evils and, if possible, for the restoration of the property—especially those slaves wch had gone off since the orders of the Spanish Court, to discountenance this practice of recg them.

Saturday, 21st.

Left Augusta about 6 o'clock, and takg, leave of the Governor & principal Gentlemen of the place at the bridge over Savanna River, where they had assembled for the purpose, I proceeded in Company with Colos. Hampton* & Taylor, & Mr. Lithgow a committee from Columbia (who had come on to meet & conduct me to that place) & a Mr. Jameson from the Village of Granby on my Rout.—Dined at a house about 20 miles from Augusta and lodged at one Odem about 20 miles farther.

*Colonel Wade Hampton, a meritorious officer in the Southern Army of the Revolution, and a commander on the northern frontier of New York in the War of 1812.

Sunday, 22nd.

Rode about 21 miles to breakfast, and) passing through the village of Granby just below the first falls in the Congaree (which was passed in a flat bottomed boat at a Rope ferry,) I lodged at

Columbia, the newly adopted Seat of the Government of South Carolina about 3 miles from it, on the No side of the River, and 27 from my breakfasting stage.

The whole Road from Augusta to Columbia is a pine barren of the worst sort, being hilly as well as poor.—This circumstance, added to the distance, length of the stages, want of water and heat of the day, foundered one of my horses very badly.

Beyond Granby 4 miles I was met by sevl. Gentlemen of that place & Wynnsborough; and on the banks of the River on the No side by a number of others, who escorted me to Columbia.

Monday, 23d.

Dined at a public dinner in the State house with a number of Gentlemen & Ladies of the Town of Columbia, & Country round about to the amt of more than 150, of which 50 or 60 were of the latter.

Tuesday, 24th. May 1791

The condition of my foundered horse obliged me to remain at this place, contrary to my intention, this day also.

Columbia is laid out upon a large scale; but, in my opinion had better been placed on the River below the falls.—It is now an uncleared wood, with very few houses in it, and those all wooden ones—The State House (which is also of wood) is a large and commodious building, but unfinished—The Town is on dry, but cannot be called high ground, and though surrounded by Piney & Sandy land is, itself good—The State house is near two miles from the River, at the confluence of the Broad River & Saluda.—From Granby the River is navigable for Craft which will, when the River is a little swelled, carry 3000 bushels of Grain—when at its usual height less, and always some.—The River from hence to the Wateree below which it takes the name of the Santee is very crooked; it being according to the computed distance near 400 miles. Columbia from Charleston is 130 miles distance.

Wednesday, May 25, 1791.

Set out at 4 o'clock for Camden—(the foundered horse being led slowly on)—breakfasted at an indifferent house 22 miles from the town, (the first we came to) and reached Camden about two o'clock, 14 miles further, when an address was reed. & answered.—Dined (late) with a number of Gentlemen and Ladies at a public dinner. The Road from Columbia to Camden, excepting a mile or two at each place, goes over the most miserable pine barren I ever saw, being quite a white sand, & very hilly.—On the Wateree within a mile & half of which the town stands the lands are very good—they Culture Corn, Tobacco & Indigo.—Vessels carrying 50 or 60 Hhds of Tobo [tobacco], come up to the Ferry at this place at which there is a Tobacco Wharehouse.

Thursday, 26th. 1791

After viewing the british works about Camden I set out for Charlotte—on my way—two miles from Town—I exammined the ground on wch. Genl. Green & Lord Rawdon had their action, 1— The ground had but just been taken by the former—was well chosen—but he not well established in it before he was attacked; which by capturing a Videt was, in some measure by surprise—Six miles further on I came to the ground where Genl. Gates & Lord Cornwallis had their Engagement wch terminated so unfavorable for the former.2 As this was a night meeting of both Armies on their march, & altogether unexpected each formed on the ground they met without any advantage in it on either side it being level & open.—Had Genl. Gates been i'2 a mile further advanced, an impenetrable Swamp would have prevented the attack which was made on him by the British Army, and afforded him time to have formed his own plans; but having no information of Lord Cornwallis's designs, and perhaps not being apprised of this advantage it was not seized by him.

Camden is a small place with appearances of some new buildings.—It was much injured by the British whilst in their possessions.

*Lord Rawdon, the British commander there, alarmed for the safety of his forts in the lower country, set fire to Camden on the 10th of May, 1781, and retreated down the Santee.*

After halting at one Sutton's 14 m from Camden I lodged at James Ingrams 12 miles farther.

Friday, 27th.

Left Ingrams about 4 o'clock, and breakfasting at one Barr's 18 miles distant lodged at Majr. Crawford's 8 miles farther—About 2 miles from this place I came to the Corner where the No. Carolina line comes to the Rd from whence the Road is the boundary for 12 miles more. At Majr. Crawfords I was met by some of the chiefs of the Catawba nation who seemed to be under apprehension that some attempts were making, or would be made to deprive them of the 40,000 Acres wch was secured to them by Treaty and wch is bounded by this Road.

*This is yet a reservation for the Catawba Indians, near the southeast corner of Yorkville district in South Carolina. It was originally larger than now. They were once a powerful tribe, but their population in 2010 was 3,370. Their chief village was on the Catawba River, about twenty-five miles from Yorkville. The following eloquent petition of Peter Harris, a Catawba warrior during the Revolution, is preserved among the Colonial records at Columbia, South Carolina. It is dated 1822:*

*"I am one of the lingering survivors of an almost extinguished race. Our graves will soon be our only habitations. I am one of the few stalks that still remain in the field where the tempest of the Revolution has passed. I fought against the British for your sake. The British have disappeared, and you are free, yet from me have the British took nothing; nor have I gained anything by their defeat. I pursued the deer for subsistence; the deer are disappearing, and I must starve. God ordained me for the forest, and my ambition is the shade. But the strength of my arm decays, and my feet fail me in the chase. The hand which fought for your liberties is now open for your relief. In my youth I bled in battle, that you might be independent! let not my heart in my old age bleed for the want of your commiseration."*

Saturday, 28th.

Set off from Crawfords by 4 o'clock and breakfasting at one Harrison's 18 miles from it got into Charlotte 13 miles further, before 3 o'clock—dined with Gen. [Thomas] Polk and a small party invited by him, at a Table prepared for the purpose.

It was not, until I had got near Barr's that I had quit the Piney and Sandy lands—nor until I had got to Crawfords before the lands took quite a different complexion—here they began to assume a very rich look.

Charlotte is a trifling place, though the Court of Mecklenburg is held in it—There is a School (called a College) in it at which, at times there has been 50 or 60 boys.

Sunday, 29th.

Left Charlotte about 7 o'clock, dined at Colo. Smiths 15 miles off, and lodged at Majr. Fifers 7 miles farther.

Monday, 30th.

At four o'clock I was out from Majr. Fifers'; and in about 10 miles at the line which divides Mecklenburgh from Rowan Counties; I met a party of horse belonging to the latter, who came from Salisbury to escort me on—(It ought to have been mentioned also that upon my entering the State of No. Carolina I was met by a Party of the Mecklenburgh horse—but these being near their homes I dismissed them)—I was also met 5 miles from Salisbury by the Mayor of the Corporation, Judge McKoy, & many others;—Mr. Stule.* Representative for the district, was so polite as to come all the way to Charlotte to meet me.—We arrived at Salisbury about 8 o'clock, to breakfast—20 miles from Captn. Fifers.—The lands between Charlotte & Salisbury are very fine, of a reddish cast and well timbered, with but very little underwood, between these two places are the first meadows I have seen on the Road since I left Virga. & here also we appear to be getting into a Wheat Country.

*General John Steele, a representative in Congress four years. He was a native of Salisbury, and first appeared in public life as a member of the North Carolina House of Commons, in 1787. He was appointed by President Washington controller of the United States Treasury, and was continued in office by President Adams. He died in 1815.

This day I foundered another of my horses.

Dined at public dinner given by the Citizens of Salisbury; & in the afternoon drank Tea at the same place with about 20 ladies who had assembled for the occasion.

Salisbury is but a small place altho' it is the County town, and the district Court is held in it;—nor does it appear to be much on the increase—there is about three hundred souls in it and tradesmen of different kinds.

Tuesday, May 31st.

Left Salisbury about 4 o'clock; at 5 miles crossed the Yadkin, the principal stream of the Pedee, and breakfasted on the No. Bank (while my Carriages & Horses were crossing) at a Mr. Youngs, fed my horses 10 miles farther, at one Reeds, and about 3 o'clock (after another halt) arrived at Salem, one of the Moravian towns 20 miles farther—In all 35 miles from Salisbury.

The road between Salisbury and Salem passes over very little good land, and much that is different; being a good deal mixed with Pine, but not sand.

Salem is a small but neat village; & like all the rest of the Moravian settlements, is governed by an excellent police—having within itself all kinds of artisans.—The number of Souls does not exceed 200.

Wednesday, June 1st. 1791.

Having received information that Governor Martin was on his way to meet me; and would be at Salem this evening, I resolved to await his arrival at this place instead of halting a day at Guilford as I had intended;

Spent the forenoon in visiting the Shops of the different Tradesmen—The houses of accommodation for the single men & Sisters of the Fraternity—& their place of worship.—Invited six of their principal people to dine with me—and in the evening went to hear them sing.—perform on a variety of instruments Church music.

In the Afternoon Governor Martin as was expected (with his Secretary) arrived.

Thursday, June 2nd. 1791

In company with the Governor I set out by four o'clock for Guilford, breakfasted at one Dobson's at the distance of eleven miles from Salem and dined at Guilford, sixteen miles farther, where there was a considerable gathering of people who had received notice of my intention to be there to-day, and came to satisfy their curiosity. On my way I examined the ground on which the action between General Greene and Lord Cornwallis commenced, and after dinner rode over that where their lines were formed and the score closed in the retreat of the American forces. The first line of which was advantageously drawn up and had the troops done their duty properly the British must have been sorely galded in ye advance, if not defeated. The lands between Salem and Guilford are in places very fine but upon the whole cannot be called more than midling, some very bad. On my approach to this place (Guilford) I was met by a party of light horse which I prevailed on the Governor to dismiss and to countermand his orders for others to attend me through the State.

Friday, 3.

Took my leave of the Governor, whose intention was to have attended me to the line, but for my request that he would not and about four o'clock I proceeded on my journey, breakfasted at Troublesome Iron Works, called fifteeen but at least is seventeen miles from Guilford, partly in the Rain and, from my information, or for want of it, was obliged to travel twelve miles further than I intended to-day, to one Gatewood's within two miles of Dix' Ferry over the Dan, at least thirty miles from the Iron works. The land over which I passed this day were of various qualities and as I approached the Dan, were a good deal covered with pine. In conversing with the Governor, on the state of politics in North Carolina I learned with pleasure that opposition to the general government and the discontent of the people were subsiding fast and that he should so soon as he received the laws which he had written to the Secretary of State for, issue his proclamation requiring all officers and members of the Government to take the oaths prescribed by law. He seems to condemn speculation in lands and the purchases from the State of Georgia, and thinks, as every sensible and disinterested man must that schemes of that sort must involve the country in trouble, perhaps in blood.

Saturday 4.

Left Mr. Gatewood's about half after six o'clock and between his house and the Ferry passed the line which divides the state of Virginia and North Carolina and dining at one Wilson's, sixteen miles from the Ferry, lodged at Halifax old Town.

The road from Dix' Ferry to Wilson passes over very hilly (and for the most part) indifferent land being a good deal mixed with pine the it is said here that pine when mixed with oak and more especially with hickory is not indicative of a poor soil. From Wilson's to Hallifax Old Town the soil is good and of a reddish cast, having this day passed the line of North Carolina and, of course finished my tour thro the three southermost states, a general description of them may be comprised in the following few words. From the Seaboard to the falls of all the rivers, which water the lands, except the swamp on the rivers and the lesser streams which empty into them and the interval land higher up the rivers is with but few exceptions neither more nor less than a continued pine barren, very thinly inhabited. The part next the Seaboard for many miles is a dead level and badly watered. That above it is hilly and not much bettter than barren, if possible less valuable on account of its hills and because they are more inconvenient to market, supposing them capable as the lands below are producing beef, pork, tar, pitch and turpentine. The lands above the falls of the several rivers from information, and as far as my own observation has extended, is of a very superior kind, from their being of a greasy red with large oaks intermixed with hickory, chestnut, etc, excelling in producing corn, tobacco, wheat, hemp and other articles in great abundance and are generally thickly inhabited, comparatively speaking with those below.

In the lower country (near the Seaboard) in the State of South Carolina and Georgia, rice as far up as the swamps extend is almost the sole article that is raised for market, some of the planters of which grow much corn as with the sweet potatoes support their people. The middle country, that is between the rice land and the falls of the rivers, and a little above them, is cultivated chiefly in

38

corn and indigo and the upper country in tobacco, Corn, hemp, and in some degree the smaller grains. It is nearly the same in North Carolina with this difference, however, that as not much rice is planted there, especially in the northern part of the state, corn, some indigo, with naval stores and pork, are substituted in its place, but as indigo is on the decline hemp, cotton, etc., are grown in its place. The inland navigation of the rivers of these three states may be improved according to the ideas I have formed of the matter to a very extensive degree to great and useful purposes and at a very moderate expense, compared with the vast utility of the measure inasmuch as the falls of most of them are trifling and their lengths are great going to the markets penetrating the country in all directions by their lateral branches and in the present state (except at the falls which, as has been observed before, are trifling)-, navigable for vessels carrying several hogheads of tobacco or other articles in proportion. The prices at which rice lands in the low parts of the state are held is very great, those of which, if have been improved from twenty pounds to thirty pounds sterling and, fifty pounds has been given for some, and from ten pounds to fifteen is the price of it in its rude state. The pine barren adjoining these sell from $1 to $2 per acre, according to circumstances.

The interval land on the rivers below the falls and above the rice swamps also command a good price but not equal to those above and the pine barrens less than those below. The lands of the upper country sell from four to six or seven dollars, according to the quality and circumstances thereof. In the upper parts of North Carolina wheat is pretty much grown and the farmers seem disposed to try hemp but the land carriage is a considerable drawback having between 200 and 300 miles to carry the produce either to Charlestown, Petersburg, or Wilmington, which are their three great marts, the of late Fayetteville receives a good deal of the bulky articles, and they are water borne from thence to Wilmington, excepting the towns and some gentlemen's seats along the road from Charlestown to Savannah there is not within view the whole road I traveled, from Petersburg to this place, a single house which has anything of an elegance appearance. They are altogether of wood, and chiefly of logs, some indeed have brick chimneys but generally the chimneys are of split sticks, filled with dirt between them. The accommodations on the whole road, except in the towns and near there, as I was informed, for I had no opportunity of judging, lodging having been provided for me in them (at my own expense) were found extremely indifferent, the houses being small and badly provided either for man or horse the extra exertions when it was known I was coming, which was generally the case, were made to receive me. It is not easy to say on which road, the one I went or the one I came, the entertainmen is most indifferent, but with truth it may be added, of course, that both are bad, and is to be accounted for from the kind of travelers which use them, which, with a few exceptions only, on the upper road, are no other than wagoners and families removing ,who generally take their provisions along with them.

The people, however, appear to have abundant means to live well. The grounds where they are settled yielding grain in abundance and the natural herbage a multitude of meat with little or no labor to provide food for the support of their stock, especially in Georgia where it is said the cattle live thru the winter without any support from the owners of them. The manners of the people, as far as my observation, and means of information extended, were orderly and civil and they appeared to be happy, contented and satisfied with the general Government, under which they were placed. Where the case was otherwise, it was not difficult to trace the cause to some demigogue or speculating character. In Georgia, the dissatisfied part of them, at the late treaty with the creek Indians were evidently land jobbers, who strangled every principle of justice to the Indians and policy to their country would, for their own immediate emolument strip the Indians of all their territory, if they could obtain the least countenance to the measure, but it is to be hoped the good sense of the state will set its face against such diabolical attempts and is also to be wished and by many it was said it might be expected that the sales by that state to what are called the Yazoo Companies would fall thru. The discontent which it was supposed the Revenue Act (commonly known by the Excise Law) would create subside as fast as the law is explained and little was said of the Banking act.

Sunday, 5th.

Left the Old Town about four o'clock A. M., and breakfasted at Pridies' (after crossing Bannister River one and a half miles) about eleven miles from it, came to Stanton River, about twelve, where meeting Col. Isaac Coles, (formerly a member of Congress for this district) and who pressing me to it, I went to his house, about one mile off to dine and to halt a day for the refreshment of myself and horses, leaving my servants and them at one of the usually indifferent taverns at the Ferry that they might be no trouble or be inconvenient to a private family.

Monday, 6th.

Finding my horses fared badly at the Ferry for want of grass and Col. Cole's kindly pressing me they were accordingly brought there to take the run of it until night. Dined with the gentlemen to-day also. The road from Halifax Old Court House or Town to Stanton River passes for the most part over this land a good deal mixed with pine.

Tuesday, 7th.

Left Col. Cole's by daybreak and breakfasted at Charlotte C. H., 15 miles, where I was detained some time to get shoes put on such horses as had lost them, proceeded afterwards to Prince Edward C. H., 20 miles further. The lands from Stanton Ferry to Charlotte C. H. are generally good and pretty thickly settled. They are cultivated chiefly in tobacco, wheat and corn with oats and flaxon. The houses, the none elegant, are generally decent and bespeak good livers being for the most part weather-boarded and shingled with brick chimneys but from Charlotte C. H. to Prince Edward C. H., the lands are of an inferior quality with few inhabitants in sight of the road. It is said they are thickly settled off it. The roads by keeping the ridges pass on the most indifferent ground.

Wednesday, the 8th.

Left Prince Edward C. H., as soon as it was well light, and breakfasted at one Treadways, 13 miles off, dined at Cumberland C. H., 14 miles further, and lodged at Moore's Tavern, within 2 miles from Carters Ferry, over James River. The road from Prince Edward C. H., to Treadway was very thickly settled, altho the land appeared thin and the growth is in a great degree pine, and from Treadway to Cumberland C. H., they were equally thickly settled, on better land, less mixed, and in places not mixed with pine. The buildings appeared to be better.

Thursday 9th.

Set off very early from Moores, but the proper ferry boat being hauled up, We were a tedious while crossing in one of the boats used in the navigation of the river, being obliged to carry one carriage at a time, without horses and crossways the boat on planks. Breakfasted at the Widow Paynes, 17 miles on the north of the river, and lodged at a Mr. Jordans, a private house, where we were kindly entertained and which we were driven to by necessity by having rode not less than 25 miles from our breakfasting stop thru very bad roads in a very sultry day without any rest and by missing the right road had got lost. From the river to the Widow Paynes and thence to Anderson's Bridge, over the North Anna Branch of the Pamonky the lands are not good nor thickly settled (except in places) from thence for several miles further but afterwards throughout the county of Louisa, which is entered after passing the bridge, the river over which it is made, dividing it from Goochland they are much better and continued so with little exception quite to Mr. Jordan's.

Friday, 10th.

Left Mr. Jordan's early and breakfasted at one Johnsons, 7 miles off. Reached Fredericksburg, after another short halt, about 3 o'clock, and dined and lodged at my sister Lewis'. The lands from Mr. Jordans to Johnson's and from thence several miles farther are good but not rich afterwards. As you approached nearer the Rappahannock River they appear to be of 'a thinner quality and more inclined to Black Jacks.

After dinner with several gentlemen, whom my sister had invited to dine with me I crossed the Rappahannock and proceeded to Stafford C. H., where I lodged. About sunrise we were off, breakfasted at Dumfrees, and arrived at Mt. Vernon for dinner.

From Monday, the 13th, until Monday, the 27th, (being the day I had appointed to meet the Commissioners, under the Residence Act, at Georgetown) I remained at home, and spent my time in daily rides to my several farms and in receiving several visits.

Monday, June 27th, 1791.

Left Mount Vernon for Georgetown before six o'clock and according to appointment met the commissioners at the place by nine, then calling together the proprietors of the lands on which the Federal City was supposed to be built, who had agreed to cede them on certain conditions at the last meeting I had with them at his place. Front some misconception with respect to the extension of their grants had refused to make conveyances and recapitulating the principles upon which my communications to them at the former meeting were made and giving some explanation of the present state of matters, and the consequences of delay in this business they readily waived their objections and agreed to convey to the uttermost extent of what was required.

Tuesday, June 28th.

Whilst the commissioners were engaged in preparing the deeds to be signed by the subscribers this afternoon I went out with Major L'Enfant and Mr. Ellicot to take more perfect view of the ground in order to decide finally on the spot on which to pce the public buildings and to direct him a line which was to leave out a spring (commonly known by the name of the Cool Spring), belonging to Major Stoddart should be run j

Wednesday, June 29th.

The deeds which remained unexecuted yesterday were signed today and the dowers of their respective wives acknowledged according to law. This being accomplished I called the several subscribers together and made known to them the spots on which I meant to place the buildings for the Executive Departments of the Government, and for the Legislature of ditto. A plan was also laid before them of the city, in order to convey to them general ideas of the city; but they were told that some alterations, deviations from it, would take place, particularly in the diagonal streets or avenues, which would not be so numerous, and in the removal of the President's house more westerly, for the advantage of higher ground. They were also told that a Townhouse or Exchange would be placed on some convenient ground between the spots designed for the public buildings before mentioned, and it was with much pleasure that a general approbation of the measure seemed to pervade the whole.

Thursday, June 30th.

The business which brought me to Georgetown being finished and the commissioners being instructed with respect to the mode of carrying the plans, into effect—I set off this morning a little after four o'clock in the prosecution of my journey towards Philadelphia, and being desirous of seeing the nature of the country north of Georgetown and along the upper road I resolved to pass through Fredericktown in Maryland and York and Lancaster in Pennsylvania, and accordingly breakfasted at a small village called Williamsburg, in which stands the Courthouse of Montgomerie County, fourteen miles from Georgetown—dined at one Peter's Tavern twenty miles further and arrived at Fredericktown about sundown, the whole distance about forty-three miles. The road by which I passed is rather hilly but the lands are good, and from Monocassy to F. T. They are well timbered. The country is better settled than I expected to find—the land is well calculated for small grain of which a good deal is now on the ground—but thin, owing, as the farmers think, to the extreme drouth of the spring, though more, as it appeared to me, to the frost and want of snow to cover their grain during the winter.

Friday, July 1st.

Received an address from the Inhabitants of Fredericktown and about seven o'clock left it. Dined at one Cookerly's thirteen miles off, and lodged at Tawnytown only twelve miles farther, being detained at the first stage by the rain and to answer the address which had been presented to me in the morning. Tawnytown is but a small place with only the street through which the road passes built on. The buildings are principally of wood. Between Cookerly's and this place we passed the little and great Pipe CPs branches of Monocacy.

44

The latter about half way between them is a considerable stream, and from its appearance capable of navigation. The lands over which we travelled this day are remarkably fine, but as was observed yesterday the fields were thinly covered with grain, owing as I conceived to the cause already mentioned. The farmhouses are good, most of them, and the settlers compact with good barns and meadows appertaining to them.

Saturday, July 2nd.

Set out a little after four o'clock and in about six miles crossed the line which divides the states of Maryland and Pennsylvania, but the trees on which are so grown up that I could not perceive the opening, though I kept a lookout for it—nine miles from Tawnytown, Littles town is passed. They are of similar appearance—buildings look more insignificant than the former. Seven miles farther we came to Hanover (commonly called McAlister-town) a very pretty village with a number of good brick houses, and mechanics in it—at this place is a good Inn—we breakfasted and in eighteen miles more we reached Yorktown, where we dined and lodged. The country from

Tawnytown to Yorktown is exceedingly pleasant, thickly inhabited and well improved. The dwelling houses, barns and meadows being good. After dinner in company with Colonel Hartley and other Gentlemen I walked through the principal streets of the Town, and drank tea at Colonel Hartley's—The C. H. was illuminated.

Sunday, July 3rd.

Received and answered an address from the inhabitants of Yorktown and there being no Episcopal minister present in the place I went to hear morning service performed in the Dutch Reformed Church which being in that language not a word of which I understood I was in no danger of becoming a proselyte to its religion by the eloquence of the preacher. After service accompanied by Colonel Hartley and a half a dozen other Gentlemen I set off for Lancaster. I dined at Wright's Ferry where I was met by General Hand and many of the principal characters of Lancaster and escorted to the town by them arriving at six o'clock. The country from York to Lancaster is very fine, thickly settled and well cultivated. About the Ferry they are extremely rich.—The River Susquehanna at this place is more than a mile wide and some pretty views on the banks of it.

Monday, July 4th, 1791.

This being the anniversary of American Independence and being kindly requested to do it I agreed to halt here this day and partake of the entertainment which was prepared for the celebration of it—In the forenoon I walked about the town. At half past two o'clock I received and answered an address from the Corporation and received the compliments of the Clergy of different denominations, dined between three and four o'clock—drank tea with Mrs. Hand.

(President Washington arrived in Phila.—Wednesday July 6th—The End of his Southern Tour.)

Tuesday, September 30th, 1794.

Having determined from the reports of the commissioners who were appointed to meet the Insurgents in the western counties in the state of Pennsylvania and from other circumstances to repair to the places appointed for the Rendezvous of the militia of New Jersey, Pennsylvania, Maryland and Virginia I left the city of Philadelphia about half past ten o'clock this forenoon, accompanied by Colonel Hamilton (Secretary of the Treasury), and my private secretary. Dined at Norristown and lodged at a place called the Trap, the first seventeen and the latter twenty-five miles from Philadelphia. At Norristown we passed a detachment of militia who were preparing to march for the Rendezvous at Carlisle, and at the Trap, late in the evening we were overtaken by Major Stagg, principal clerk in the Department of War, with letters from General Wayne and the western army, containing official and pleasing accounts of his engagement with the Indians near the British post at the Rapids of the Miami of the Lake, and of his having destroyed all the Indian settlements on that River in the vicinity of the said post quite up to the grand Glaize, the quantity was not less than 5000 acres (?) and the stores, etc., of Col. McGee, the British Agent of Indian affairs, a mile or two from the Garrison.

October 1st (Wednesday)

Left the Trap early and breakfasting at Pott's Grove, eleven miles we reached Reading to dinner 18 (?) miles farther where we found several detachments of Infantry and Calvary preparing for their march to Carlisle.

Thursday, October 2nd.

An accident happening to one of my horses occasioned my setting out later than was intended. I got off in time, however, to make a halt to bait my horses at Womeldorfs fourteen miles, and to view the Canal from My era-town towards Lebanon and the Locks between the two places, which (four adjoining each other in the dissent (descent) from the Summit ground) along the Tulpehocken; built of brick,) appeared admirably constructed. Reached Lebanon at night—twenty-eight miles.

Friday, October 3rd.

Breakfasted at Humel's T. fourteen miles and dined and lodged at Harrisburg on the banks of the Susquehanna, twenty-three miles from Lebanon. At Harrisburg we found the First Regiment of New Jersey (about 560 strong)1 commanded by Colo Turner, drawn out to receive me. Passed along the line to my quarters and after dinner walked through and round the town, which is considerable for its age (of about eight or nine years). The Susquehanna at this place abounds in Rockfish of twelve or fifteen inches in length, and a fish which they call Salmon.

Saturday, October 4th.

Forded the Susquehanna nearly a mile wide including the island at the lower end of which the road crosses it. On the Cumberland side I found a detachment of the Philadelphia Light Horse ready to receive and escort me to Carlisle, seventeen miles; where I arrived about eleven o'clock—two miles short of it I met the Governors of Pennsylvania and New Jersey with all the Cavalry that had Rendevouzed at that place drawn up, passed them, and the Infantry of Pennsylvania before I alighted at my quarters.

Sunday, October 5th.

Went to the Presbyterian meeting, and heard Dr. Davidson preach a political sermon, recommendation of order and good government and the excellencies of that of the United States.

October 6th—12th.

Employed in organizing the several detachments which had come in from different counties of the state in a very disjointed and loose manner, or rather I ought to have said in urging and assisting Gen. Mifflin to do it as I no otherwise took the command of the troops than to press them forward and to provide them with necessaries for their march as well and as far as our means would admit. To effect these purposes I appointed Gen. Hand, Adjutant General, on the 7th.—On the 9th William Tindley and David Reddick deputed by the Committee of Safety (as it is designated) which met on the 2nd of this month at Parkinson Ferry arrived in Camp with the Resolutions of the said Committee, and to give information of the state of things in the four western couties of Pennsylvania, to wit: Washington, Fayette, Westmoreland, and Alleghany, to see if it would prevent the march of the army into them. At ten o'clock I had a meeting with these persons in presence of Governor Howell (of New Jersey,) the Secretary of the Treasury, Col. Hamilton, and Mr. Dandridge— Governor Mifflin was invited to be present but excused himself on account of business.

I told the deputies that by one of the Resolutions it would appear that they were empowered to give information of the disposition and of the existing state of matters in the four countries above mentioned; that I was ready to hear and would listen patiently and with candour to what they had to say. Mr. Tindley began.—He confined his information to such partsof the four counties as he was best acquainted with, referring to Mr. Reddick for a recital of what fell within his knowledge in the other parts of these countries. The substance of Mr. Tindley's communications were as follows, viz: that the people in the parts where he was best acquainted had seen their folly and he believed were disposed to submit to the Laws; that he thought but could not undertake to be responsible for the re-establishment of the public offices, for the collection of the taxes on distilled spirits and stills, intimating, however, that it might be best for the present or until the people's minds were a little more tranquilized to hold the office of inspection at Pittsburg, under the protection or at least under the influence of the Garrison; that he thought the distillers would either enter their stills or would pull (?) them down; that the civil authority was beginning to recover its tone;—and enumerated some instances of it; that the ignorance and general want of informatiom among the people far exceeded anything he had any conception of!—that it was not merely the Excise Law that opposition was aimed at, but to all Law and Government and to the officers of Government; and that the situation in which he had been and the life he had led for some time was such that rather than go through it again he would prefer quitting this scene altogether. Mr. Redick's information was similar to the above except to the three last recitals, on which I do not recollect that he expressed any sentiment further than that the situation of those who were not in the opposition to Government whilst the frenzy was at its height were obliged to sleep with their arm* by their bedside every night; not knowing but that before morning they might have occasion to use them in defense of their persons or their properties. He added that for a long time after the riots commenced and until lately the distrust of one another was such that even friends were afraid to communicate their sentiments to each other; that by whispers, this was brought about; and growing bolder as they became more communicative they found their strength; and that there was a general disposition not only to aquiesce under but to support the Laws; and he gave some instances also of Magistrates enforcing them. He said the people of those counties believed that the opposition to the Excise Law, or at least that their dereliction to it in every other part of the United States was similar to their own, and that no troops could be got to march against them for the purpose of coercion:—that every account until very lately of the troops marching against them was disbelieved, and supposed to be the fabricated tales of governmental men;—that now they had got alarmed;—that many were disposing of their property at an under rate in order to leave the country; and added, (I think), that they would go to Detroit;—that no persons of any consequence, except one, but what had availed themselves of the proffered

49

amnesty;—that those who were still in the opposition and obnoxious to the Laws were men of little or no property, and cared but little where they resided;—that he did not believe there was the least intention in them to oppose the army; and that there was not three rounds of ammunition for them in all the western country.—He, (and I think Mr. Tindley also)-, was apprehensive that the resentments of the army might be productive of treatment to some of these people that might be attended with disagreeable consequences and on that account seemed to deprecate the march of it: declaring, however, that it was their wish that if the people did not give proofs of unequivocal submission that it might not stop short of its object. After hearing what both had to say I briefly told them that it had been the earnest wish of Government to bring the people of those counties to a sense of their duty by mild and lenient means; that for the purpose of representing ' to their sober reflection the fatal consequences of such conduct commissioners had been sent amongst them that they might be warned in time of what must follow if y ' they persevered in their opposition to the Laws; but that by coercion would not be resorted to except in the *dernier* resort, but that the season of the year made it indispensable that the preparation for it should keep pace with the proposition that had been made; that it was necessary for me to enumerate the tranactions of those people, (as they related to the proceedings of the Government) , for as much as they knew them as well as I did; that the measures which they were now a witness to the adoption of was not less painful than expensive; was inconvenient and distressing in every point of view, but as I considered the support of the Laws as an object of the first magnitude and the greatest part of the expense had already been incurred, that nothing short of the most unequivocal proofs of absolute submission should retard the march of the army into the western counties in order to convince them that the Government could and would enforce obedience to the Laws not suffering them to be insulted with impunity: being asked again what proof would be required, I answered, they knew as well as I did what was due to justice and example. They understood my meaning and asked if they might have another interview. I appointed five o'clock in the afternoon for it.

At this second meeting there was little more than a repetition of what had passed in the forenoon; and it being again mentioned that all the principal characters except one in the western counties who had been' in the opposition had submitted to the proposition I was induced, seeing them in the street the next day, to ask Mr. Redick who that one was, telling him, at the same time, I required no disclosure that he did not feel himself entirely free to make. He requested a little time to think of it, and asked for another meeting which was appointed at five o'clock in that afternoon when it took place accordingly, when he said David Bradford was the person he had alluded to in his former conversation. He requested to know if a meeting of the people by their deputies would be permitted by the army at any given point on their march into that country (with fresh eveidence of the sincerity of their disposition to aquiesce in whatever might be required.) I replied; "I saw no objection to it provided they came unarmed, but to be cautious that not a gun was fired, as there could be no answering for consequences in this case. I assured them that every possible care should be taken to keep the troops from offering them any insult or damage, and that those who always had beeen subordinate to the laws and such as had availed themselves of the amnesty should not be injured in their persons or property; and that the treatment of the rest would depend upon their own conduct; that the army unless opposed did not mean to act as executioners or bring offenders to a military Tribunal, but merely to aid the civil magistrates with whom offences would lie. Thus ended the matter. On the 10th the Light and legionary corps under the immediate command of Major McPherson, the Jersey Regiment and Guimey's from Philadelphia commenced their march under the orders of Governor Howell, and the day following the whole body of Cavalry (except the three troops of Philadelphia Horse commanded by Captain Dunlap as part of the Legion above mentioned), and under Gen. White, a new formed corps of independent uniform companies and several other corps under the command of Gov. Mifflin marched all for the rendezvous at Bedford. The rank of the principal officers of the army being first settled by me as follows: First, Governor Lee of Virginia, to be commander in chief, if I do not go out myself; second Governor Mifflin, third

Governor Howell, fourth Maj. General Daniel Morgan, or Major General Irvine, according to the dates of their militia commissions; the brigadiers in like manner according to seniority.

October 12th.

Having settled these, matters I set the troops off as before mentioned, given them their route and day's marching, and left Major General Irvine to organize the remainder of the Pennsylvania detachments as they might come in and to march them and the Jersey troops on when refreshed. I set out from Carlisle about seven o'clock this morning, dined at Shippensburg, twenty-one miles, and lodged at Chambersburg eleven miles farther, when I was joined by the Adjutant General, Hand.

October 13th.

Breakfasted at Greencastle, ten miles, and lodged at Williamsport fourteen miles farther. Having now passed through the states of Pennsylvania and Maryland, Williamsport being on the banks of the Potomac at the mouth of the Conogocheagan (?) I shall summarily notice the kind of land and state of improvement along the road I have come. From the city of Philadelphia, or rather from Norristown to Reading the road passes over a reddish and slaty or shelly kind of land through a very open and hilly country, tolerably well cultivated by the farmers. The farmhouses are good, and their barns above mediocrity, the former chiefly of stone. The whole road indeed from Philadelphia to Reading goes over hilly and broken ground but very pleasant, notwithstanding. From Reading to Lebanon along what is called the Valley, the country is extremely fine, the lands rich, the agriculture good, as the buildings also are, especially the barns which are large and fine and for the most part of stone. This settlement is chiefly of Dutch and upon the Tulpahockon. From Lebanon to Harrisburg, along the same vale, the lands are also good, but not in so high a state of cultivation as between Reading and Lebanon. From Harrisburg to Carlisle the lands are exceedingly fine, but not under such cultivation and improvement as one might have expected. From Carlisle along the left road, which I pursued to be out of the march of the army and to avoid the inconvenience of passing the waggons belonging to it, the lands are but indifferent, until we came to within a few miles of Shippensburg. The first part being of a thin and dry soil succeeded by piney flats (not far from the South Mountain. For a few miles before we arrived at Shippensburg the lands were good but uncultivated. The improvements along this road were mean. The farms scattered, the houses but indifferent, and the husbandry apparently bad. Along the road which the Troops marched both lands and the improvments, I was told, are much better. The roads come together again at the eastern end of the town. From Shippensburg to Chambersburgh the road passed over pretty good land, better (but not well) cultivated than that bteween Carlisle and Shippensburg. From Chambersburg o Williamsport the lands are fine, the houses an improvement amended considerably.

October 14th.

About seven o'clock, or half after it, we left Williamsport, and travelling upon the Maryland side of the River we breakfasted at one—, 13 miles on our way, & crossing the Potomac a mile or two below Hancock Town, lodged at the Warm Springs or Bath, 16 miles from our breakfasting stage, and 29 from Williamsport.

October 15th.

Left Bath by seven o'clock, & crossing the Cacaphon (?) Mountain & the Potomack River by a very rough road, we breakfasted at one Golders—distant about 7 miles—Bated our horses at a very indifferent place ab't 13 Miles further on, and lodged at the Old Town 33 or 34 Miles. This distance, from the extreme badness of the Road, more than half of it being very hilly, & great part of it stony, was a severe days journey for the carriage horses—they performed it however, well.—

October 16th.

After an early breakfast we set out for Cumberland and about 11 o'clock arrived there.—Three Miles from the Town was met by a party of Horse, under the command of Major Lewis (my nephew) and by Brig'r Gen'l Smith, of the Maryland line, who escorted me to the camp, where, finding all the Troops under arms, I passed along the line of the army, & was conducted to a house, the residence of

Major Lynn of the Maryland line (an old Continental Officer) where I was well lodged, & civily entertained.—

October 17th & 18th.

Remained at Cumberland, in order to acquire a true knowledge of the strength, condition &ca of the Troops, and to see how they were provided, and when they could be in readiness to proceed. I found upwards of 3200 men (officers included) in this Encampment— understood that about 500 more were at a little village on the Virginia side, 11 miles distant, calleed Frankfort, under the command of Maj'r Gen'l Morgan; that 700 men had arrived at that place the evening of the 18th, under Brig'r Mathews, and 500 men were expected in the course of a few days under Colo Page; and that the whole were well supplied with provisions, forage & Straw.

Having requested that everything might be speedily arranged for a forward movement, and a light corps to be organized for the advance under the command of Major Gen'l Morgan, I resolved to proceed to Bedford next morn'ng. At this place a deputation was received from the County of Fayette consisting of a Colo Mason, Terrence and Clinton, who came to give assurance that deposits for the army might safely be made in that County, and any person sent from it for this purpose would be safe in doing it. They were desired to get their wheat ground up and their oats threshed out, to be in readiness to be drawn to any place, or places, that might be required after the army had crossed the mountains. From Colo Mason (who has beeen a uniform friend to Government) and from a variety of concurrent accounts, it appears evident that the people in the Western Counties of this state have got very much alarmed at the approach of the army; but though submission is professed, their principles remain the same, and that nothing but coercion & example will reclaim & bring them to a due & unequivocal submission to the Laws.

October 19th.

In company with Gen'l Lee, who I requested to attend me, that all the arrangements necessary for the army's crossing the Mount'ns in two columns might be made, their routs & days marches fixed, that the whole might move in unison—and accompanied by the Adjutant General and my own family we set out ab't eight o'clock for Bedford, and making one halt at the distance of 12 miles, reached it a little after 4 o'clock in the afternoon, being met a little out of the encampment by Gov'r Mifflin, Gov' Howell & several other officers of distinction. Quarters were provided for me at the House of a Mr. Espy, Proth-onotary of the County of Bedford, to which I was carried and lodged very comfortably. The Road from Cumbel'd to this place is, in places, stoney, but in other respects not bad.—It passes through a valley the whole way, and was opened by Troops under my command in the Autumn of 1758.—The whole vallley consists of good farming land, & part of it, next Cumberland, is tolerably well improved in its culture but not much so in Houses.

October 20th.

Called the Quarter Master General, Adjutant General, Contractor, & others of the staff departm't before me, & the Commander in chief, at nine o'clock this morning, in order to fix on the Routs of the two columns & their stages: and to know what the situation of matters were in their respective departments, and when they w'd be able to put the army in motion; also to obtain a correct return of the strength and to press the commanding officers of corps to prepare with all the celerity in their power for a forward movement. Upon comparing accts it was found that the army could be put in motion 23rd, and it was so ordered by the Routs which will be mentioned hereafter. Matters being thus arrang'd I wrote a farewell address to the army, through the Commander in Chief, Gov'r Lee, to be published in orders and having prepared his Instructions and made every arrangment that occured as necessary I prepared for my return to Philadelphia, in order to meet Congress, and to attend to the Civil duties of my Office. I should have mentioned before that I found (on my arrival at Bedford) the judge and attorney for the district of Pennsylvania attending, as they had been required to do, the army. I found also, which appeared to me to be an unlucky measure, that the former had issued his warrants against, and a party of light horse had 'actually siez'd, one Herman Husbands and one Tilson (?) as Insurgents, or abettors of the Insurrection—I call it unlucky because my intention was to have suspended all proceeding of a civil nature until the army had united its columns in the center of the Insurgent counties & then have ciezed at one & the same all the leaders and principals of the Insurrection—and because it is to be feared that the proceeding above mentioned will have given the alarm, and those who are most obnoxious to punishment will flee from the Country.

So therefore I came home—to Richmond—

(The President & his Suite arrived in Phila—from Bedford—Oct. 28, 1794.)

(April, 1795)

Tuesday 14th. Left Philadelphia for Mt. Vernon, 14 reached Wilmington.
15. Ditto —Roger's Susqs.
16. Baltimore.
17. Bladensburgh.
18. Georgetown.
19. Mount Vernon, and remained there until the 26th.
26. Came to Georgetown.
27. In the federal City.
28. Arrived at Bladensburgh.
29. Baltimore.
30. Roger's—Susquehanna.

(May, 1795)

May 1st came to Wilmington.
2. Arrived at Philadelphia.

(July, 1795)

15. Left Philaa with Mrs. Washington and my family for Mt. Vernon.
Dined at Chester and lodged at Wilmington.
16. Breakfasted at Christa—dined at Elkton and lodg'd at Susquehanna—One of my horses overcome with heat.—
17. Breakfasted before I set out—dined at Hartford and lodged at Websters—bro't on the sick horse led.

18. Breakfasted in Baltime—dined and lodged at Spurriers where my sick horse died.—

19. Breakfasted at Vanhornes—dined at Bladensburgh and lodged in Geo. Town.

20. After doing business with the Comrs of the fed'l City I proceeded on my journey and got home to dinner.

For August (1795)

6. Left home on my return to Philadelphia—met the Potok Co at Geo: Town and lodged there.

7. Breakfasted at Bladensburgh—din'd at Vanhornes and lodged at Spur'rs.

8. Breakfasted at Baltimore and dined and lodged at Webster's.

9. Breakfasted at Hartford, dined at Susquehanna and lodged at Charlestown.

10. Breakfasted at Elkton, dined at Newcastle and lodged at Wilmington.

11. Breakfasted at Chester and dined in Phil'a.

For September (1795)

8. Left Phil'a for Mt. Vernon—dined at Chester and lodged at Wilmington.

9. Breakfasted at Christianna, dined at Elkton and lodged at Charlestown. -

10. Breakfasted at Susquehanna (Mrs. Roger's) dined at Hartford and lodged at Websters.—

11. Breakfasted at Baltimore—dined and lodged at Spurriers.

12. Breakfasted at Van Horns—Dined at Bladensburgh and Lodged at George Town and reached Mt. Vernon to dinner.

Sept. 25th. Went to Alexandria.—dined with Mr. [Tobias] and Mrs. Lear.

26th Returned home to dinner.

For October (1795)

12. Set out for Phil'a.

13. Stayed at Geo' Town.

14. Lodged at Spurriers.

16. Lodged at Websters.

17. Ditto at Hartford.

18. Ditto at Elkton.

19 Ditto at Wilmington.

20. Arrived at Phil.

The whole month of November has been remarkable pleasant—The ground has never been froze—but few white frosts, and no Snow.—

January 1798—December 1798 Remarks in January.

2. Clear with the Wind (tho' not much of it) at N'o

W't—Mer ab't 30.—A Mr. Elliott came to dinn'r and stayed all night.

3. Mrs. L. Washington and Mr. Elliott went away after breakfast, and Mrs. Washington, myself &ca went to Alexandria and dined with Mr. Fitzhugh—Morning clear but lowering afterwards—Mer. about 28. Wind N'o easterly.

8. Wind at S'o E't in the Morning and lowering—Mer—at 28—ab't. Noon it began to rain and cont'd to do so all the aftern'n—Mer. 30 at Night—A Mr. Marshall Music Master came here—Tuned Nelly Custis'* Harpsicord and returned after dinner.

*Eleanor (Nelly) Parke Custis (1779-1852), daughter of John Parke "Jacky" Custis, Martha Washington's son by her first marriage.—Ed. 2016

11. Clear with the wind fresh all the forenoon from No' W't—Mer at 25 in the Morn'g.—36 at its greatest Height and 27 at Night—Mr. Lear dined here and returned.

14. A little lowering all day with but little wind and that Southerly. Mer at 36 in the Morning, 46 at Night and 48 when highest. Mr. Lewis Burwell came to dinner and Mr. Woodward in the evening.

15. Southerly Wind-Soft Monn'g—thin clouds—Mer at 46 at Sunrise—50 at Noon and 50 at Night—Slow rain from 12 o'clock with the wind Southerly—Mr. Burwell and Mr. Woodward went away and I went to Alexandria to a meeting of the Stockholders of that Bank to an election of Directors.

20. Still likely for Snow—a small sprinkle, but not enough to cover the ground in the Morning.—About 10 o'clock it cleared and became remarkably pleasant—wind Southerly—Mer at 26 in the Morning—40 at highest,. and 32 at Night.—Mr. G. W. Craik came here to dinner.

23. Snow just sufft to cover the ground, fell in the night—Wind at N'o W't in the morning and Mer at 30 noon 25, and at night 20.—Wind fresh all day.—Mr. Howell Lewis came to dinner.

24. Wind at N'o W't in the morning—at noon 28—and at Night 22.—Clear all day, and afternoon the Wind was Southerly—Mr. J'no Hopkins and Mr. Hodgden came to dinner.

25. Wind Southerly all day and much like Snow in the forenoon—clear afterwards—Mer. 26—32 and 32.—Messrs. Hopkins and Hodgden went away after Breakfast.

28. Snow about an inch deep—Clear and wind at N'o W't and Mer at 20 in the morning.—33 at its highest and 20 at Night—Mr. Craik and Mr. Howell Lewis went away after breakfast.

February—1798.

1. Clear wind about S'o W't and Mer. 28 in the Morning.—Pretty brisk from N'o W't about Noon—and Calm towards night and clear all day—Mer. 40 at Night and 45 when highest—A Mr. Lad and a Mr. Gibbes from Rhode Island dined here and returned to Alexandria.

3. Wind brisk from N'o W't and Mer. 42 in the Morning—Clear and but little of it afterwards—Mer 44 at highest and 38 at Night. A Mr. Adamson from Hamburgh and Doct'r Stuart came to dinner.

4. Wind Southerly and weather lowering—Mer at 31 in the Morning, 44 at Noon and at Night, afternoon clear. Mr. Adamson went away after breakfast—and Mr. Craik and Mr. Marshall came to dinner, the latter returned after it.

5. Clear all day and wind ceasing towards

Night—Dr. Stuart went away after breakfast.

7. Wind Southerly in the Morning but shifted before 10 o'clock and turned very cold. Mer. 31 in the morn'g. Went to a meet'g of the

Potomak Co in George Town—Dined at Col'o Fitzgeralds and lodged at Mr. T. Peters.

8. Visited the Public build'g's in the Morn'g. Met the Comp'y at the Union Tavern and dined there—lodged as before. Weather very cold. Wind Northerly.

9. Returned home to Dinner—hard freezing the three last Nights—Weather still cold— Found Mr. Geo. Calvert here.

10. Mr. Calvert left this breakfast.

12. Clear. Went with the family to a Ball in Alexa given by the Citizens of it and its vicinity in commemoration of the anniversary of my birthday.

14. Wind at N'o and Mer. 25 in the morning—clear afterw'ds. Mer. 33 at Night.—Mr. Alex'r Spotswood and Wife and Mr. Field'g Lewis and Mr. Lear came to dinner, the latter returned afterwards.

15. Afternoon clear and evening lowering.—

Mr. Field'g Lewis went away after dinner.

16. Cloudy most part of the day. Mr. and Mrs. Spotwood left us after breakfast.

18. —Mer. 24 at Night and 34 at highest. Doct'r

Stuart came in the evening.

19. Mer at 22 in the morning—Wind at N'o E't and extremely cloudy—about four o'clock it began to Hail. Doct'r Stuart went away after Break't.

March 1798

3. Cloudy with appearances of Snow. Wind at N'o a little Easterly. Mer. 29 and ground frozen in the morning—ab't noon it cleared and the wind shifted to the Southward—Mer. 30 at Night and 34 at highest—Mr. G. W. Craik dined here and returned.

4. Morning clear and calm—White frost—Mer. 26—gr'd frozen—Clear and pleasant all day with the Wind at S'o. Mer. 41 at night and 43 at highest. Doct'r Stuart came to dinner.

5. Calm Morn'g with Indications of a change in the weather—Mer at 30. Doct'r Stuart left this, to accompany Washington Custis to St. Johns College at Annapolis.—Mess'rs Bonne and Lawrence from New York and young Hartshorn dined here and ret'd. Mer. 40, at N. 46.

6. Morning clear Doct'r Craik dined here and went away afterwards.

8. Cloudy with the wind at N'o E't, but not much of it and Mer at 40 in the Mom'g—Clear afterwards and wind Southerly Col'o Heth, Col'o Fitzgerald and Mr. Paller dined here—the two last left it after dinner.

9. Morning—sun rose red—thin gauz clouds—Wind N'o E't. Mer. 38—Clear afterwards and wind at S'o W't. Mer. 50 at Night, 52 at height. Colo. Heath went away after breakfast.

10. Morning clear and smoaky—Wind at South and Mer at 50— Clear all day and wind in same quarter Ludwell and Geo. Lee Esq'rs and Mr. Robert Beverly dined here and returned and Mr. and Mrs. Peter and Nelly Custis came after dinner.

11. Morning—thin clouds—brisk South wind. Mer at 57.—in the afternoon Rain with thunder and lightening—Mer at 55 and 63 at highest. Col'o Ball and Doct'r Stuart came to Dinner.

12. Clear all day—Mer. 42 at Night and

44 at highest—Calm evening—Col'o Ball and Dr. Stuart went after B't.

13. Morning cloudy and but little wind—Mer at 40—

Clear afterw'rds Mr. Peter went away after break.

17. Morning cloudy—Wind at East and Mer at 35

Mr. Snow of Massachusetts dined here and returned to Alex'a.

18. Morning thick Mr. Steer, Sen'r and Jun'r,

Miss Steer and Mrs. Vanhaven dined here and returned to Alex'a afterwards. Mr. Peter came in the afternoon.

19. Morning—Raining slow Mer. 42 at Night and no higher all day. Homs of the New Moon up.—Dined with Mrs. Washington ec'a at Mr. Thomson Mason's.

20. Mr. Law'e Washington of Chotanck and Mr. Law'e Washington of Belmont came to Dinner. Al-bin Rawlins came to live with me as Clerk.

21. Mr. L. Washington of Belmont went away.

23. Mr. L. Washington of Chotanck and Mr. Peter went away after breakfast.

25.— Mr. Nichols and wife and Mr. Lear and family dined here. Mr. Peter return'd.

27. —Mr. Charles Carroll, Jun., and Mr. Will'm Lee came to dinner

28. —Mr. Carroll and Mr. Lee went away after brekafast and the family here went to dine with Mr. Nichols.

30. —Doct'r Flood dined here.

31. A Mr. Tevot, a French Gentleman recom'd by Count de Rochambeau dined here and a Mr. Freeman, Member in Congress from N. Hamp came in the afternoon and returned.

(April—1798)-

1. Morning smoaky and a little cloudy, with the wind fresh from the Southward. Mer. 60—at night 66, and not higher all day. Mr. Law, a Mr. Taylor, Lieut't Walton of the Navy and young Mr. Barry came to dinner, and Ch's Alexander, Jun'r came at night.

2. Morning, very heavy, wind at N'o E't, Mer. 56—Raining more or less from 10 ocl'k, wind more Northerly—Mer 40 at night. Mr. Law and the Gentlemen who came with left this about noon.

4. Morning very thick and misting Mr. Alexander went away after breakfast.

8. Morning—Began to rain about 6 o'clock and became a fine clear day with the wind moderately from N'o W't——Cap. John Spotwood and Mr. Lear came to dinner—the last went after it.

9. Mr. Peter went away after breakfast, leav- ing Mrs. Peter behind him.

12. Mr. Peter ret.

13 Gen'l Lee came to dinner and Col'o Heath and son in the aftern'n.

14. Gen'l Lee and Col'o., Heath went away after breakfast and Dr. Stuart came to D.

15. Mrs. Fitzhugh and her daughters and son came in the afternoon.

16. Doct'r Stuart went away. I went to Alex'a to an Election of Delegates for the C'ty of Fairfax—voted for Mess'rs West and Jno. Herbert—returned to dinner. Mr. Fitzhugh came in the Afternoon.

17. Morning—Wind at No Wt and disagreeably Cold. Mer at 28. Clear and cold all day—A very severe frost—ground hard frozen—Ice sufficient to bear—Fruit supposed to be all killed—leaves of trees bit, etc. Mer. 36 at Night—37 highest.

18. Morning—Clear and more moderate—Wind still at No Wt. Mercury at 32—Clear all day and but little Wind after Morn'g. Mer. 50 at Night and no higher all day. Peaches not killed and hoped other fruit not hurt. Points of New Moon upwards. Mr. Fitzhugh and family left this after breakfast.—Began to plant corn at Union farm.

20. Mr. Peter went away after breakfast and Mr. Townsend and Mr. Nich's Fitzhugh came to Din.

21. Mr. Dade and Mr. Fitz'h went after breakf.

22. Doct'r Craik came on a Visit to Eleanor Peter.

23. Mr. Peter returned—sent for

24. Doct'r Craik came in the afternoon to visit Mr. Peter's Children.

25. —Doct'r went away after breakfast.

26. Morning very heavy—Wind at S. E. Mer. 53—Clear afterwards and turning very warm. Mer at 67 at Night and not higher all day.

The Rev'd Mr. Fairfax and Doct'r Craik (to visit Mr. Peter's children) came to dinner—the first returned afterwards.

27. Doct'r Craik went away after breakfast and Mr. and Mrs. Law and a Mr. Ghan, a Sweedish Gentleman came to dinner.

29. Mr. Ghan w't away after breakfast.

30. Morning Clear, wind Southerly, Mer at 62, 70 at Night and 74 at highest—Mr. Law and Mr. Peter went after breakfast and Doct'r Craik and Mrs. Craik and Son, Mr. and Mrs. Harrison and Mrs. Jenifer and a Miss Barnes came to dinner and returned afterwards.

May 1798.

2. A light sprinkling of Rain and Cloudy in the morning—Mer. 66—clear afterwards and very warm—Mer 71 at Night and 75 at highest. Mr. Law returned to din'r.

4. Morning—Clear and wind Southerly—Mer at 66. Appearance of Rain but none fell Mr. and Mrs. Law went away after breakfast and Nelly Custis went up to Hope Park.

6. A Mr Taylor and a Mr. Crips introduced by Mr. Potts dined here as did Mr. S. Peter and Mr. Lear. All except Mr. Peter went away after dinner.

8. Morning perfectly clear and pleasant—Calm-j-Mer at 64.— Lowering afternoon. Mr. Peter, Mrs. Peter and their children left this and the Rev'd Mr. Lewis from Connecticut came in the Afternoon.

9. Mr. Lewis went awiay after breakfast—I went to the Procla'n Sermon in Alexandria.

13. Mr. White and Doct'r Craik dined here, the latter went away after din'r.

14. Morning—clear and cool. Calm. Mer at 49—Some appearances of Rain ab't noon but they went off—wind No. Et and Mer at 60 at Night. Mr. White left after breakfast.

18. Clear Morning—no rain fell—clear all day—Mer at 60 in the morning and 66 at Night—Horns, or points of the Moon upwards.—

19. Morning—Clear—wind Southerly and Mer at 55.—About 8 O'clock in the forenoon Mrs. Washington and Myself sat out on a visit to Hope Park and the Federal City—Got to the former to dinner and remained there until Morning when we proceeded to the City.

Dined at Mr. Thos. Peter's and remained there until Wednesday, and then went to Mr. Law's and remained there until Friday when we sat out on our return home and called at Mount Eagle to take our leave of the Rev'd Mr. Fairfax who was on the point of embarking for England.

25. Mrs. Peaks fam dined here.

27. Mr. Lear dined here.

29. Went up to Alex'a on business and returned home to dinneer.

30. Col'o Morris, Lady & 4 Children came here after dinner.

31 Col'o Morris & family left this after breakfast

—and Mr. Herbert & Son, the Rev'd Mr. Addison, a Mr. Rogers of Baltimore, Mr. Delivs (?) of Bremen & a Mr. Pekmoller of Hamburgh dined here & returned afterwards.

June—1798.

1. Morning—clear & pleasant—Wind Southerly & Mer at 62—Cloudy more or less all day—Mer. 70 at Night. Mr. Hartshorne & Mr. Lear dined here.

2. Mr. Law & a Polish Gentleman, the Companion of General Kosciaski came here to dinner, as did Miss Lee of Greenspring with Nelly Custis who return'd today.

3. Mrs. Law came down to dinner & Mr. & Mrs. McClanahan dined here & returned afterwa'ds.

6. Mr. Law went away this morning & Dr. Stuart, Mrs. Stuart & three daughters came to breakfast & dinner.

10. Doct'r Stuart returned & Mr. Lear dined here.

*Tobias Lear was Washington's personal secretary. See Letters & Recollections of George Washington from Lear's collection.—Ed. 2016*

11. Mr. Tracy came in the evening.

12. Mr. Law returned in the Evening.

13. Mr. Fitzhugh, Lady, & daughter, Mrs. Beverley Randolph, with her daughter & Son in Law Randolph & his Sister dined here.

14. Mrs. Stuart & her family & Mr. Law, Mrs. Law and Mr. Niemcewitz (the Polish Gent'n) went away after breakfast.

15. Mrs. Lund Washington dined here.

17.—Mr.—sent by Mr. Pearce to attend my Cradlers in harvest arrived.

21. Mr. Lear & Mr. Tracey dined here—the first re- turned afterwards.

22. Mr. Tracey went away dinner.

26. Mr. Law & two French Gent'n, viz—Mr. La Guin & Mr. Clarmont.

28th. Col. Simm dined here.—

July—1798.

1. Morning—Clear & wind Southerly. Mer. 74.—Day clear & very warm. Mer. 86 at Noon & 84 at night—Mr. Fitzhugh of Chatham & Doct'r Welford dined here—as did Dr. Field.

3. Mrs. Fairfax,* her Sister, daughter & widow Price, Mrs.—, Mr. Ferd'd Fairfax & Lady, and Mr. John Herbert & his two Sisters dined here & returned.

*Not Sally Fairfax, the great love of Washington's life. She had gone to England in 1773 with her husband.—Ed. 2016

4. Morning clear—Breeze from the N'o but light—Mer. 78.80 at Night—Went up to the Celebration of the Anniversary of Independence and dined in the Spring Gardens near Alex'a with a large Compa of the Civil & Military of Fairfax County.

6. Doctors Thornton & Dalson, Mr. Ludwell Lee, Lady & Miss Armistead, & Mr. David Randolph & a Son of Colo R. Kidder Mead

came here to Dinner, the the two last proceeded to Alex'a afterwards.

7. —Mr. R. Bland Lee & Mr. Hodgden came here to dinner & Mr. Ludwell Lee & Lady went away after Din.

8. —Mr. Lee & Miss Portia Lee, Mr. Hodgden, & Doct'r Stuart who came in the afternoon of yesterday went away after breakfast & Mr. & Mrs. Potts, Miss Fitzhugh, Mrs. Conway, Miss Brown, Mr. Wm. Wilson, Mr. Wm. Ramsay & Mr. Lear came to Dinner & returned.

10.—Doct'r Craik, Wife & Son—a Mr. Craik of Alex'a & Mrs Hunter of Baltimore—Mr. Jno. Herbert—Mr. De Bourg, Presid of the College at George Town, an- other of the Professors & two of the Stud'ts, viz—a son of Mr. Laws & a Neph of Barrys dined here & all ret'd.

11. Mr. Fitzhugh & his oldest daughter dined here— he went away afterwards & Mr. McHenry, Sect'y of War came in the evening.

12. The following Comp'y dined here. Colos Fitz- gerald & Simms, Mr. Herbert & Son—Doct'r Craik & Son—Mr. L. Lee, Col Ramsey— Cap. Young & L't Jones, Mr. Potts, Wm. Wilson, Mr. Porter, Doct'r, Cook, Mr. Riddle, Mr. Lear, Mr. Tracey—& six Ladies & 4 Gent'n from Mr. Rogers.

15. Mr. Law dined here & returned afterw'ds.

17 Mr. & Mrs. Fitzhugh & their younger daughter & son & Mr. Lear came to dinner, the last retu'd after.

18. Mr. Fitzhugh & all his family went away after dinner.

19. Miss Digges & her niece, Miss Carroll dined here.

20. Went up to Alex'a with Mrs. W. & Miss Custis—Dined at Doct'r Craiks, ret'd in ye aftn.

22. Mr. Mrs. Dalton & their two daughters came here to dinner.

23. Mr. Lear came in the M'g—stayed all day.

24. —Doct'r Stuart & Mr. Geo. Graham dined here, the last went away afterwards.

25. This family & Mr. Dalton's di'd [dined]with Mr. Lee.

26. Mr. Herbert, wife, 2 daughters, son & Mr. & Mrs. Whiting dined here—as did the Count Inznar & Mr. Merchant.—all went aw

29. Doct'r Craik din'd h

31. Mr. L. Washington—Mr. Foot & a Maj'r Parker dined here and returned.

August—1798.

2. Morning clear and calm—Mer at 74. Clear all day—Wind Southerly—M. 80 at Night—Mr. Lear dined here & Mrs. Washington of Bushfield & her G. daughter, Ann Wash'n came in the Aftem'n.

5. Wash'n Custis came home f'm [from] College.

6. Went to Alex'a to a meeting of the Pot'o Co. Mr. Bur: (Burwell) Bassett came home with me.

7. Mr. Lear & the boys dined here & with Mr. Bas- sett went afterward.

9. Doct'r Stuart came to dinner.

10 Mr. & Mrs. Thornton & Jno Herbert & G. W. Craik came to dinner, the two last returned.

11. Gen'l & Mrs. & Miss Spotswood & two younger daughters came in afternoon.

14. Mr. Booker came in the aftern'n.

15. Mr. & Mrs. Ludwell & Miss Armstead & Mr. Fielding Lewis dined here & returned.

16. Colo Simms & Lady, & Mr. Herbert & Son dined here.

17. Mr. Tracey came in the Morn'g & Mr. Harper at Night.

18. Mr. Tracy went away after dinner & Mr. Booker in the Morn'g.

20. Mr. Harper went away after Breakfast.

No acc't kept of the weather &c from hence to the end of the Month—on acc't of my Sickness which commenced with a fever no the 19th & lasted until the 24th, which left me debilitated.—

On the 28th there was a very refreshing Rain but not suff't to go to the Roots of Indian Corn which was suffering very much for want of it.—

September—1798

2. Mr. White came to dinner.

3. In the Morning to breakfast came Gen'l Marshall & Mr. Bushrod Washington*—and to dinner the At'y Gen'l Chas Lee, Mr. Herbert, Mr. Keith & Doc. Craik—the last went away.

*Associate Justice of the Supreme Court of the United States.—Ed. 2016

4. In the Afternoon Mr. & Mrs. Parks of Frederiskb'g came here.

5. —Gen'l Marshall & Mr. B, Washington went to a dinner in Alex'a given to the former by the Citizen's there & returned.

6. Mr. Marshall & Mr. B. Washington went away before breakfast Mr. Wm Craik came to breakfast & returned afterwards, and Mr. Jno. Herbert & Mr. Rob't Burwell came to dinner—the latter returned after it—the former stayed all Night.

7. Mr. Herbert went after dinner.

8. Mr. & Mrs. Parks left this after breakfast.

13. Mrs. Fairfax and daughter—Miss Dennison and a Mrs. Tibbies dined here.

15. Mr. White came to dinner.

16. Doct'r Stuart & Doc'r Craik came to dinner— day warm.

17. Mr. White & Doctors went away this morning.

19. Doct'r Craik came in the Morning to visit Mr. L. Lewis & stayed all day & Night.

20. Went up to the Federal City—Dined & Lodg'd at Mr. Thos. Peters.

21. Examined in company with the Com'rs some of the Lots in the Vicinity of the Capital & fixed upon No. 16, in 634 to build on. Dined & lodged at Mr. Laws.

22. Came home with Mr. T. Peter, wife & 2 Children to Dinner—Mer at 70 at Night and evening cool.

23. Mr. & Mrs. Nichols & his brother & Mr. Swan- wick dined here.

25. Mr. Geo. Steptoe Washington who came to din- ner yesterday returned today—& Mr. Peter set off for New Kent—Mer. 64 at Noon and 58 at Night.

26. Mr. Tracey came here to dinner.

27. Mr. Jno. Herbert came to dinner—and a Major Simons of Charleston in the aftern'n.

28. Maj'r Simons went away in the Morning & Mr. Herbert & Mr. Tracy in the afternoon.

30. Morning clear & calm—Mer at 44—clear all day. Went to Church in Alex'a. Mer. 59 at Night.

October—1798

4. Mr. Jno. Herbert & Mr. G. W. Craik dined here & Capt: Jno. Spotswood came in the evening.

5. Doct'r Thornton, Mr. Law and a Mr. Baldo, a Spanish Gentleman from the Havanna came to Dinner.

6. Mr. Bushrod Washington & Capt'n Blackburn came to dinner & Mr. Thos. Peter returned in the afternoon from New Kent.

7. Mr. B. Washington & Capt'n Blackburn went away after Breakf't.

10. and eleventh absent—in the Federal City—Weather warm & dry the whole time.—M. Welch & Mr. Tracey came in the afternoon.—

12. Mr. Welch & Mr. Tracey went in the Forenoon & Mr. Wm. Craik came to dinner.

13. Gen'l Lee, Capt'n Presley Thornton & Mr. Peters came to dinner. Wd. Easter

14. Gen'l Lee & Capt'n Thornton went away after breakfast & Mr. Booker came at Night.

16. The Attorney Gen'l of the United States Lee and Lady & Mr. Wm. Craik dined here & ret'd.

17. Mr. Law—a Mr. David Barry and a Mr. Sheddon came to dinner & staid the Night.

18. Mr. Law & his Company went away after breakfast.

24. —Mrs. Washington, Mrs. Peake and Doctor Stuart dined here, the two first went away afterwards. M. 56 at Night.

25. Doct'r Stuart & Mr. Booker went away after breakfast. M. 65 at N.

26. Mr. & Mrs. Law, with Gov'r Crawford (late of Burmuda) & Lady came to dinner.

28. The Att'y Gen'l U. S., Mr. Jno. Hopkin & Mr. Ch's. T. Mercer dined here & returned.

29. Mr. & Mrs. Law, Mr. & Mrs. Peter and Gov'r Crawford & Lady all went after breakfast.

31. Doct'r Craik visited Patients at Union farm & dined here.

November 1798.

2. Mr. Law, Mr. Hasler of Demarrara & Lady came to dinner.

4 Clear—but Cool. Mr. Fitzhugh, Mr. David Randolph & Mr. Alex'r White came to dinner, & the two first went away afterwards—Mr. Hasler & Lady went away after breakfast & Mrs. Law came at Night.

5. Mr. White went away before brekfast—I set out on a journey to Phila., about 9 o'clock with Mr. Lear my Secretary—was met at the Turnpike by a party of horse & escorted to the Ferry at George Town where I was rec'd with Military honors—lodged at Mr. T. Peters.

6. Breakfasted at Bladensburgh—dined & lodged at Spurriers. Escorted by horse.

7. Breakfasted at Baltimore—dined at Websters, & lodged at Hartford—Met at Spurriers by the Baltimore horse & escorted in and out by the same—Viewed a Brigade of Militia at Balt'e.

8. Breakfasted at Susquehanna escorted by the Hartford horse—dined at Elkton and lodged at Christiana br'dge.

9. Breakfasted in Wilmington & dined & lodged at Chester—wait'g at the latter the Return of an Exp's at this place was met by sev'l Troops of Phil'a horse.

10. With this Escort I arrived in the City about 9 o'clock & was rec'd by Gen'l McPhersons Blues & was escorted to my lodgings in 8th Street (Mrs. White's) by them & the Horse.

11. 12, & 13 dined at my Lodgings receiving many Visits—Weather clear & pleasant.

14. Dined at Maj'r Jacksons.

15. Dined at Mr. Tench Francis's. Rain at Night.

16. Dined at the Seecret'y of the Trea'y.

17. Ditto at Mr. Willings.—

18. Ditto at My lodgings—Weather cloudy and heavy.

19. Ditto at Doct'r Whites—Bishop—Raining.

20. Dined at the Secretary of Wars—Violent Snow Storm from No Et

21. Dined at Maj'r Reeds—Senator's.

22. Dined at Mr. Binghams.

23. Ditto at Mr. Sam'l Meridiths, Treasurer.

24. Ditto at the Secretary of States.

25. Ditto at my Lodgings.

26. Dined at the Presidents of the U. States.

27. Dined in a family with Mr. Morris.

28. Dined with Judge Peters.

29. Ditto with the British Minister.

30. Ditto with the Gov'r of the State, Gov'r Mifflin.

December (1798)

1. Dined with Mr. Rawle.

2. Ditto with Bingham. From hence until my leaving the City on the

13. I dined at my lodgings.

14. After dinner set out on my journey home.—Reached Chester.

15. Breakfasted at Wilmington, bated at Christiana—and dined and lodged at Elkton.—

16. Set out after a very early breakfast; and was detained at Susquehanna from 10 o'clock until the next morning—partly by Ice and Winds—but principally by the Lowness of the tides occasioned by the No Westerly Winds.

17. Breakfasted at Barneys—Bated at Hartford—Dined at Websters and lodged at Baltimore.

18. Breakfasted at Spurriers—dined at Rhodes's and lodged at Mr. Laws in the Federal City.

19. Stopped at Doct'r Thorntons and Mr. Peter's & dined at home. Snow having fallen about 3 inches deep in the night.—

24th. Doct'r Craik came to D. & Judge Cushing & lady in the Afternoon—As did a Mr. Dinsmoor, Agent in the Cherokee country on his way to Philadelphia—with a Mr

25. Gen'l Pinckney, Lady & daughter came to dinner, and Captain Jno. Spotwood in the Afternoon.

27. Clear morning, but spitting of snow in the Evening, little however fell. Mer at 25 in the Morning*

28. Gen'l Pinckney, Lady & daughter left this after breakfast.

January 1799

23. Lowering—Mer at 40. Wind (tho' but very little of it) Southerly. Lowering through the day.—Mr. Bush-rod Washington' came to dinner.

25. Doct'r Stuart & family & Mr. Bush'd Wash'n went away after breakfast.

February 1799.

7. Clear & pleasant all day—Mer at 20 in the Morning—but little Wind and that Easterly—Doct'r Thorn, and

Mas'r Turner came to dinner.

8. Mr. Thos. Digges dined here & returned. Mr. Tracy came to dinner.

9. Thornton & Turner went away ab't Noon.

11. Went up to Alexandria to the celebration of my birthday—Many manoevers were performed by the Uniform Corps, and an elegant Ball & supper at night.

12. Wind westerly and day clear and pleasant. Returned home—Mr. N. Fitzhugh & brother & Mr. Thos. Wash'n came to dinner.

16. Mr. & Mrs. Peters came to dinner.

18. Mrs. Stuart and her 3 daughters came here in the afternoon.

20. Doct'r Baynham dined here.

21. Mr. Ch's Carter, wife & daughter came to dinner & Mr. Robt. Lewis in the afternoon.

22. Morning raining—Mrc at 30—

24. The Rev'd Mr. Davis & Mr. Geo. Calvert came to dinner, & Miss Custis was married ab't Candlelight to Mr. Lawrence Lewis.

25. Clear & very cold in the Morning, and through the day—Mer at 12 in the morning and 22 at night. Wind at No Wt. River nearly closed with Ice.—Mr. L. Lee, Mrs. Lee & Miss French—Mr. Herbert, Mr. Jno. Herbert & Miss Herbert, Doca'r Craik & Mr. G. W. Craik, Miss Fitzhugh, Miss Moly Fitzhugh & Miss Chew & Colo Fitzgerald dined here & returned.

26 Mrs. Potts, Mrs. Fendall, Mr. And'w Ramsay & wife, Mr. Wm. Ramsey Mr. Edm'd Lee & sister Lucy, and Mr. Hodgden dined here & returned, and Mr. Bush-rod Washington came in the afternoon.

27. Mr. Thomson Mason & wife, and Mr. Nicholls & wife dined here & returned.

March 1799.

3. Mrs. Stuart & her 3 daughters (Stuarts ( and Mr.

& Mrs. Peters went away after breakfast.

4. Mr. & Mrs. Carter went away after Breakfast.

5. Mr. Law'e Lewis & wife went up to the Fed'l City.

6. Mr. & Mrs. Law went away today.

8. Mr. Mrs. & Miss Carter returned this afternoon.

9. Morning clear but lowering, and at times raining through the day. Major Pinckney came in the Evening.

10. Mr. Carter & family and Major Pinckney left this after breakfast, and young Mr. Barry with a Spanish Officer, a Mr. O'Higgens came to dinner and returned afterwards.

16. A Mr. Boyd & his Brother from Boston din'd here.

23. Mr. & Mrs. Law'e Lewis returned from the Federal City [later Washington D.C.].

24. Mr. Robt. Stith came to dinner & stayed all N.

25. Doct'r Craik & Mr. Foot dined here & returned in the afternoon.

26. Mr. Stith went away after breakfast.

29. Mr. Burwell Bassett came in the Evening.

31. Mr. Bassett went away after breakfast.

April 1799.

3. Extreme cold (but forgot to see what the mercury was). Wind very high from No Wt, and continued so all day.—Went up to Four Mile Run to run round my land. They got on the g'rd about 10 o'clock and in Company with Capt'n Steer and Mr. Luke commenced the survey on 4 Mile Run & ran agreeably to the Notes taken. In the evening went to Alex'a and lodged myself at Mr. Fitzhughs.

4. Recommenced the survey at the upper end and where we left off, in company with Colo Little, Capt'n Steer (?) and Mr. Will'm Adams & count'd it agreeably to the notes until we came to 4 Mile Run again which employed us until dark.—Returned to Alex'a and again lodged at Mr. Fitzhughs.

5. Returned home to Breakfast.

6. Mr. White, the Fed'l Commd came to dinner and Colo Ball after dinner.

8. Colo Ball & Mr. White went after breakfast.

9 Mrs. Washington at Home.

11. Mr. Foot dined here, & with Mrs. Washington returned home in the afternoon.

12. Doct'r Wade came this aft'n. Spread Plaster of Paris this morning on the circle & sides before the door & on the Lawn to the cross Path betwn the Garden gates & on the clover by the stable.

17. Mr. Tayloe, Esq'r & Mr. Jno. Herbert came here to dinner.

18. Mr. Tayloe & Mr. Jno. Herbert went away after breakfast.

20. Mrs. Washington, of Hayfield, Gen'l O'Donald, Mr. Barry, Mr. Oliver, Mr. Thompson & a Doct'r dined here & returned.

21. A Mr. B. Happesley Coxe, Esq'r recom'd by Mr. Bingham (?) came here to dinn'r.

22. Mr. Coxe went away after breakfast & Mr. Van Statherst (?) came to dinner, & Dr. Craik to see Mr. Lear afterwards.

23 Doct'r Craik went away before breakfast & a Maj'r Jones, a british officer came to dinner & Mr. George Peter at night.

24. Gentlemen who came yesterday went away after breakfast and I went up to Alex'a to an Election of a Representative from the District to Congress, & from the County to the State Legisla'e.

25. Doct'r Stuart came to dinner.

26. Doct'r Stuart went away after breakfast and Mr.

& Mrs. Lawrence Lewis came from Hope Park in the afternoon.

28. Doct'r Craik & a Mr. Halsted dined here & re- turned.

29. Went up to run round my land on 4 Mile Run. Lodged at Colo Littles.

30. Engaged in the same business as yesterday & returned home in the afternoon

May 1799.

3. Messrs Wm. L. Washington and a Mr. Jeffries dined here & returned.

6. Mr. & Mrs. Lewis set out on their journey.

9. Gen'l Lee, Messrs R. B. Lee & Wm. Ludwell Lee, Mr. Fitzhugh, Mr. Page & Mr. T. Turner dined here & returned in the Evening.

10. Mr. Thos. Digges & Jas Welch dined here & ret'd.

11. Doct'r Stuart came to dinner & a Mr. Small afterwards—Both stayed at night. '

12. Doct'r Stuart went away after Breakfast & Mr. Short after dinner—Mr. White came to dinner.

13. Mr. White went away before breakfast.

14. Maj'r Wm. Harrison came here to dinner.

15. Mr. Thomson Mason came here to breakfast and attended Maj'r Harrison & me on the survey of the letters land, & both dined here as did a Mr. Season (?)

16. Went up to Alexandria to the Purse Race & re- turned in the Evening. Mr. Law & Doct'r Thornton here.

18. A Mr. Boies & Lady, from Boston dined here & returned to Alex'a.

19. Mr. Peak, Miss Eaglin (?) & a Mr. Brent dined here and went away afterwards, as did Mr. Law & Doc. Thornton.

20 A Mr. Hancock from Boston & a Mr. Smith from Portsmouth dined here.

21. Mr. Fitzhugh & two daughters, Mr. Mrs. & Miss Turner, Messrs.. W. & Washington Craik & Mr. Jno. Herbert dined here—the last & Mr. Turner's family stayed the night.

22. Mr. Mrs. & Miss Turner and Mr. Herbert went away after breakfast.

23. Mr. Thos. Adams, third son to the President, & Mr Joshua Johnson, Lady & son came to din'r.

24. Col. Ball came to breakfast, and went away after dinner.—Mr. T. Peter & Mrs. Peter & young Powell came to dinner.

25. All the company except Mr. & Mrs. Peter went away after breakfast.

26. Mr. & Mrs. Peter went away after breakfast.—Mr. & Mrs. Nichols came to dinner & Maj'r Geo. Lewis & Doct'r Welford came in the afternoon.

27. Capt'n Presley Thornton & Lady came to dinner as did Mr. Lear,

28. All the strangers went away after breakfast.

31. Went up to the Fed'l City—dined & lodged with Mr. Peter.

June 1799.

1. Dined and lodged at Mr. Laws.

2. Returned home to dinner—tak'g church at Alex'a in my way. Found Doct'r Stuart here.

3. Doct'r Stuart went away after Breakfast.

5. A Mr. Ch's. Newbald from New Jersey dined here & went away afterwards.

9. Mr. Alex'r White came to dinner.

10. Mr. Page & Mr. Selden dined here, & went away afterwa'ds.

11. Bishop Carroll, Mr. Digges & his sister Carroll, Mr. Page & Doct'r Craik all dined here.

13. Mrs. & Miss Fairfax & Miss Dennison dined here.

15. Capt'n Geo. S. Washington & Mr. Robt. Lewis came in the afternoon.

16. Dcot'r & Mrs. Stuart & their 3 daughters came here to dinner.

17. Capt'n Washington & Mr. Lewis went away early this morning, & Doct'r Stuart aft.

18. Mrs. Washington came to dinner.

19. Mrs. & Miss Fairfax & Mr. Donaldson and Mr. Foote came to Dinner and went away afterwards, as did Mrs. Washington.

20. The following company dined here—Chief-Jus- tice of the U. S. Ellsworth, Mr. & Mrs. Steer, Sen'r, Mr. & Mrs. Steer, Jun'r Mr. Van Havre, Mr. & Mrs. Ludwell Lee, Mrs. Corbin Washington, Mr. & Mrs. Hodgson & Miss Cora Lee, Mr. & Mrs. Geo. Calvert and a Cap'n Hamilton & Lady from the Bahama Islands.

22. Dr. Stuart's family & Mr. & Mrs. Calvert went away after breakfast.

July 1799.

1. Doct'r Tazewell & Mr. Burwell Bullett came to dinner.

2. Doct'r Tazewell & Mr. Bullett went away in the morning, & a Capt'n Moore, from the East Indies & a Mr. Teal (?) from Phila came to dinner & returned to Alex'a in the afternoon.

3. Doct'r Stuart & a Parson Laltum (?) from Penn- sylvania dined here & left it in the afternoon.

4. Went up to Alex'a and dined with a number of the citizens there in celebration of the anniversary of the Declaration of American Independ'ce at Kemps Tavern.

6. Doctors Tazewell & Thornton came in the evening.

7. Mr. Will'm Booker came in the evening.

9. Doctors Tazewell & Thornton went away before breakfast.

10. Mr. & Mrs. Law & a Mr. Dunn came here to din- ner.

12. Doct'r Tazewell & Mr. G. W. Craik came here in the afternoon. Mr. Booker went away.

14. Gov. (?) Lee & Mr. W. Craik dined here—Doct'r Tazewell went away after dinner.

16. Mr. Dunn left this after breakfast.

17. Colonels Powell & Simms and Mr. Herbert and Judge Washington, Capt'n Blackburn & Mr. H. Turner dined here.—The three first went away in the afternoon.

18. Capt'n Blackburn went away after breakfast.

19. Judge Washington & Mr. H. Turner left this after dinner.

20. Mr. Law went away after breakfast.

22. Mr. Law returned this afternoon.

23. Mr. Needham Washington came in the afternoon.

25. Very little wind, and very warm, but being unwell, no acc't was taken of the Mer.—Visited by Doct'r Craik.

26. Doct'r Craik went away after breakf'st.

30 A Major Riddle (a British officer), Colo Fitzgerald, & Mr. James Patton and Mr. B. Bassett came to dinner. The first three went away afterw'ds.

August 1799

2—Capt'n Blue of the Am'n [American] army who came here yesterday to dinner returned today after breakf.

4. Dcot'r Stuart & his brother Richard & Mr. Foot dined here & returned afterwards.

5. Clear & warm—Went up to George Town, to a general meeting of the Potomac Company—dined at the Union Tavern and lodged at Mr. Law's.

6. Clear & warm—returned home to dinner—found Gen'l Wm. Washington of So. Carolina & son here—Wind Southerly.

7. The following Gentlemen dined here, viz: Colo Fitzgerald, Doct'r Craik & son, Mr. Wm. Craik, Mr. Herbert & son, Jno. C. Herbert, Colo Ramsey, Mr. Potts, Mr. Edm'd Lee, Mr. Keith, Lieut. Kean of the Marines and Mr. Chas. Fenton Mercer.

8. General Washington & Son went away after breakfast & Dr. & Mrs. Jenifer came to dinner.

9. Doct'r & Mrs. Jenifer went away after break- fast, as did Mrs. Law, Mr. Law hav'g left it on Monday last.

15. Mr. Thomas Digges dined here.

16. Young Mr. McCarty dined here.

23 Mr. & Mrs. Lav' came here to Dinner.

24. Mr. White came to dinner, as did 4 Gentlemen from Phila., viz: young Mr. Meridith (son of the Treasurer) Mr. Clifton, a Mr. Walter &—-,the 4 last returned after dinner.

31. Morning clear—Mer at 76. Calm—82 at highest & 78 Night. Messrs. Willm. & George Craik dined here & returned.

September 1799

1. A brisk Southerly wind in the Morning—clear—& Mer at 70 and at night 83, Cloud, thunder & lightning & Rain to the northward of us, but none fell here. Doct'r Craik dined here—sent for to Mrs. Washington who was sick.

3. Mrs. Washington & her Dr., of Bushfield & B. Washington & Wife, & Dr. Stuart came in.

5. —Doct'r Stuart went away after breakfast.

6. Mr. B. W. & wife went after breakfast—Doct'r Craik, who was sent for in the night to Mrs. Washington, came early this morning.

7. Mr. & Mrs. Peter and Gen'l Washington came in the afternoon. Gen'l Washington went away after breakfast & Mr. & Mrs. Law came to dinner.

10. Mrs. Washington & her grand-daughter went away after breakfast—Doct'r Stuart came to dinner, & Doct'r Craik (sent for)'came in the afternoon.

11. Doctors Craik & Stuart, & Mr. Peter went away after breakfast.

12. Capt'n Truxton came to dinner.

13. Mr. & Mrs. Law went away after breakfast & Doctor Thornton came to dinner.

17. Doct'r Thornton went away after breakfast & Mr. Thos. Peter & his brother Lieut't Peter came to Dinner.

18. Mr. George Peter went away after breakf't.

20. Mr. Ludwell Lee and Messrs. Stanton & Parker from the Eastern shore of Virginia and a Mr. Hilton dined here & went away afterwards.

21. Mr. Alex. White came to dinner.

23. Mr. Alex White went away after B—.

24. Mr. Thos. Peter went away after breakfast.

25. Mrs. & Miss Fairfax & Miss Dennison dined here & returned & Doct'r Stuart came in the Evening.

27. Governor Davie on his way to the Northward to Embark as Envoy to France called, dined & Proceeded on. Mr. T. Peter came.

29. Doct'r Craik came to dinner on a visit to Mrs. Washington & stayed all night.

30. Doct'r Craik went after Breakf'.

October 1799.

1. Mrs. Fairfax, sister & daughter, & Mrs. Herbert & Mrs. Nelson, Mr. Jno. Herbert & two of Wm. Washington of Fairfields sons dined here. Mrs. Fairfax &ca went away after dinner—the others remained.

2. Mrs. Herbert, Mrs. Nelson &ca went away.

4. Mrs. Peak dined here and in the Afternoon Colo Jno. Walker & Mr. Hugh Nelson came here.

7. Mr. Peter went to Geo. Town this Mom'g.

9. Colo Walker & Mr. Nelson set out for the City of Washington after breakfast.

10. Mr. T. Peter returned to night.

12. Mr. Mrs. Peter & family went away after breakfast & Mr. Law's Lewis and his wife came to dinner.

24. Mrs. Swanwick (?) dined here.—Mrs. Stuart & family went up to Alex.

25. Mr. & Mrs. Liston and Mr. Gilman left this after breakfast, and Mr. Law'e Washington, Junior, came here at night.

26. Doct'r Stuart & family and young McCarty re- turned here to Dinner.

27. Doct'r Stuart & family and Mr. Law'e Washington & young McCarty all went away after breakfast,

28. A Mr. Ridout, an English Gentleman and his Lady dined here as did Mr. G. W. Craik. Mr. Lear set out for Harpers Ferry to make some arrangement with Colo Parker respecting cantoning the Troops.

29. Colo Griffen, Mr. Law and a Mr. Valangin (an

Eng'h Gentleman introduced by Mr. Barthw Dan- dridge—) the latter went away afterwards.

31. Colo Griffen & Mr. Law went away after break- fast, and Mr. William Craik came here in the Aftern'n.

November 1799

1 Mr. Craik went away after Breakfast—Mer. 49 at night.

2. Mr. Jno. Fairfax, formerly an overseer of mine, came here before dinner and stayed all night.

3. Morning cloudy—Wind at No Et & Mer at 42.—Clear evening. Mer at 42. Mr. Valangin came to dinner..

November 1799.

4. A Mr. Teakle from Accomack County dined here & returned as did Doct'r Craik.—Mr. Lear returned from Berkley.

5. Morning and the whole day calm, clear & pleasant.—Set out on a trip to Difficult-run to view some Land I had there, & some belonging to Mr. Jno. Gill, who had offered it to me in discharge of

Rent which he was owing me.—Dined at Mr. Nicholas Fitzhugh's and lodged at Mr. Corbin Washington's.

6. Set out from thence after 8 o'clock, being detained by sprinkling Rain, & much appearance of it until that hour—reached Wiley's Tavern near Difficult Bridge to Breakfast, and then proceeded to survey my own Land, the day clearing and the weather becoming pleasant.

7. Weather remarkably fine—finished surveying my own Tract & the Land belonging to Gill, returning as the night before to Wiley's Tavern.

8. Morning very heavy and about 9 o'clock it commenced Raining, which it continued to do steadily through the day—notwithstanding which I proceeded to ascertain by actual measurment the qualities. This being finished betw. 12 & 1 Oclock I returned to Wiley's Tavern & stayed there the remainder of the day,

9. Morning & whole day clear, warm & pleasant. Set out a little after 8 O'clock—Viewed my biulding in the Fed'l City.—Dined at Mr. Law's & lodged at Mr. Thos. Peter's.

10. Still remarkably fine, clear & pleasant—Wind Southerly— Returned home about Noon.—Mr. Law, Mr. Barry, Mr. White & Doct'r Thornton came to dinner & stayed at night.

11 The Gentlemen above mentioned went away after breakf't.

14. Mr. Valangen came to dinner & stayed all night.

15. Rode to visit Mr. now Lord Fairfax, who was just get'g home from a trip to England. Ret'd to dinner.

16. Doct'r Craik came here in the afternoon on a visit to sick people.

17. A very heavy and thick fog—Morning calm, & Mer at 41. About 2 Oclock the Sun came out and the afternoon was pleasant.—Went to Church in Alexandria & dined with Mr. Fitzhugh. On my return f'd young Mr. McCarty here on his way back from the Federal City. Young McCarty came to Din'r.

20. Mr. McCarty went away after breakfast, and Mrs. Summers, Midwife for Mrs. Lewis came here abt 3 o'cl'k.

21. Mrs. Stuart & the two eldest Miss Stuarts came here to dinner.

22. Colo Carrington & lady came in the aftern'n.

23. Colo Carrington & Lady went away after Break- fast—Doct'r Craik came to dinner & Doct'r Stuart at Night.

25. Doct'r Craik & Doct'r Stuart both went away after Breakfast.

27 Doct'r Craik who was sent for to Mrs. Lewis (& who was delivered of a daughter ab't — o'clock in the forenoon came to Breakfast & stayed dinner—Mr. Dublois dined here, and both went away afterwards.

28 Colo & Mrs. Carrington came to Dinner.

29 Young D. McCarty came to dinner and Mr. Howell Lewis & wife after dinner.

30. Colo & Mrs. Carrington went away after B'f.

December 1799.

I. Mr. Foot dined here.

2. Lord Fairfax & Lady, Daughter & Miss Dennison dined here.

3. Mrs. Stuart & daughters went away after breakfast.

7. Dined at Lord Fairfax's.

9. Mr. Howell Lewis & wife set off on their return home after breakfast—and Mr. Lawe Lewis and Washington Custis on a journey to—(?)

11. But little wind and Raining—Mer at 44 in the morning and 38 at Night.—About 9 Oclock the Wind shifted to No Wt & it ceased raining but continued cloudy.—Lord Fairfax, his son Thos and daughter, Mrs. Warren ' (?) Washington & son, Whiting, and Mr. Jno. Herbert dined here and returned after dinner.

13. Morning snowing and ab't 3 Inches deep. Wind at No. Et. & Mer at 30. Cont'd snowing till 1 Oclock, and ab't 4 it became

perfectly clear—Wind in the same place but not hard. Mer. 28 at Night.

(General Washington died the following day.)

# APPENDIX

*This rare letter of President Washington is here presented by the courtesy of Mr. Martin F. Douglas, of Greensboro, N. C.*

Mount Vernon, May 20th, 1792.

My dear Sir.

As there is a possibility if not a probability, that I shall not see you on your return home!—or, if I should see you that it may be on the road and under circumstances which will prevent my speaking to you on the subject we last conversed upon; I take the liberty of committing to paper the following thoughts, & requests.

I have not been unmindful of the sentiments expressed by you in the conversations just alluded to:—on the contrary I have again, and again revolved them, with thoughful anxiety; but without being able to dispose my mind to a longer continuation in the office I have now the honor to hold.—I therefore still look forward to the fulfillment of my fondest and most ardent wishes to spend the remainder of my days (which I cannot expect will be many) in ease & tranquility.

Nothing short of conviction that my deriliction of the Chair of Government (if it should be the desire of the people to continue me in it) would involve the Country in serious disputes respecting the chief magistrate, & the disagreeable consequence* which might result therefrom in the floating, & divided opinions which seem to prevail at present, could, in any wise, induce me to relinquish the determination I have formed: and of this I do not see how any evidence can be obtained previous to the Election.—My vanity, I am sure is not of that cast as to allow me to view the subject in this light.

Under these impressions, then, permit me to reiterate the request I made to you at our last meeting—namely—to think of the proper time, and best mode of anouncing the intention; and that you would prepare the latter.—In revolving this subject myself, my judgment has always been embarrassed.—On the one hand, a previous declaration to retire not only carries with it the appearance of vanity & self importance, but it may be construed into a manoeuvre to be invited to remain.—And on the other hand, to say nothing, implys

87

consent; or at any rate, would leave the matter in doubt; and to decline afterwards might be d'eemed as bad, & uncandid.

I would fain carry my request to you farther than is asked above, although I am sensible that your compliance with it must add to your trouble; but as the recess may afford you leisure, and I flatter myself you have dispositions to oblige me, I will, without apology desire (if the measure in itself should strike you as proper, & likely to produce public good, or private honor) that you would turn your thoughts to a valedictory address from me to the public, expressing in plain and modest terms—that having been honored with the Presidential Chair, and to the best of my abilities contributed to the Organization & Administration of the government—that having arrived at a period of life when the private walks of it, in the shade of retirement, becomes necessary and will be most pleasing to me;—and the spirit of the government may render a rotation in the Elective Officers of it more congenial with their ideas of liberty & safety, that I take my leave of them as a public man;—and in bidding them adieu (retaining no other concern than such as will arise from fervent wishes for the prosperity of my Country) I take the liberty at my departure from civil, as I formerly did at my military exit to invoke a continuation of the blessings of Providence upon it—and upon all those who are the supporters of its interests, and the promoters of harmony, order & good government.

That to impress these things it might, among other things be observed, that we are all the children of the same country—a country great and rich in itself—capable, & promising to be, as prosperous and happy as any the Annals of history have ever brought to our view—That our interest, however deversified in local & smaller matters is the same in all the great & essential concerns of the Nation:—That the extent of our Country—the diversity of our climate & soil—and the various productions of the States consequent of both, are such as to make one part not only convenient, but perhaps indispensably necessary to the other parts:—and may render the whole (at no distant period) one of the most independent in the world:—That the established government being the work of our own hands, with the seeds of amendment engrafted in the

Constitution, may by wisdom, good dispositions, and mutual allowances, aided by experience, bring it as near to perfection as any human institution ever aproximated; and therefore, the only strife among us ought to be, who should be foremost in facilitating & finally accomplishing such great & desirable objects; by giving every possible support, & cement to the Union.—That however necessary it may be to keep a watchful eye over public servants, & public measures yet there ought to be limits to it; for suspicions unfounded, and jealousies too lively, are irritating to honest feelings, and oftentimes are productive of more evil than good.

To enumerate the various subjects which might be introduced into such an address would require thought; and to mention them to you would be unnecessary, as your own judgment will comprehend all that will be proper; whether to touch, specifically, any of the exceptionable parts of the Constitution may be doubted.—All I shall add therefore at present, is, to beg the favor of you to consider—1st the propriety of such an address.—2d if approved, the several matters which ought to be contained in it—and 3d the time it should appear: that is, whether at the declaration of my intention to withdraw from the service of the public—or to let it be the closing act of my administration—which, will end with the next Session of Congress (the probability being that that body will contiue sitting until March.) when the House of Representatives will also dissolve.—

Though I do not wish to hurry you (the cases not pressing,) in the execution of either of the publications before mentioned, yet I should be glad to hear from you generally on both—and to receive them in time, if you should not come to Philadelphia until the Session commences, in the form they are finally to take.—I beg leave to draw your attention also to such things as you shall conceive fit subjects for communication on that occasion; and noting them as they occur that you would be so good as to furnish me with them in time to be prepared and engrafted with others for the opening of the Session—

With very sincere and

Affectionate regard

I am—ever Yours

Go Washington.

James Madison, Junr, Esqr.

THE END

Discover more lost history from BIG BYTE BOOKS

Made in the USA
Coppell, TX
01 December 2024